DIRECTORY OF BRITISH RAILWAYS

DIRECTORY OF BRITISH RAILWAYS

NEW AND REOPENED STATIONS
1948–2018

PAUL SMITH AND SALLY SALMON

PEN & SWORD TRANSPORT

AN IMPRINT OF PEN & SWORD BOOKS LTD
YORKSHIRE - PHILADELPHIA

First published in Great Britain in 2019 by
Pen and Sword Transport
An imprint of
Pen & Sword Books Ltd
Yorkshire - Philadelphia

ISBN 978 1 52670 430 6

A CIP catalogue record for this book is available from the British Library.

Typeset in 10/12 Gill Sans
By Aura Technology and Software Services, India

Printed and bound in India by Replika Press Pvt. Ltd.

Pen & Sword Books Ltd incorporates the Imprints of Pen & Sword Books Archaeology, Atlas, Aviation, Battleground, Discovery, Family History, History, Maritime, Military, Naval, Politics, Railways, Select, Transport, True Crime, Fiction, Frontline Books, Leo Cooper, Praetorian Press, Seaforth Publishing, Wharncliffe and White Owl.

For a complete list of Pen & Sword titles please contact

PEN & SWORD BOOKS LIMITED
47 Church Street, Barnsley, South Yorkshire, S70 2AS, England
E-mail: enquiries@pen-and-sword.co.uk
Website: www.pen-and-sword.co.uk

or

PEN AND SWORD BOOKS
1950 Lawrence Rd, Havertown, PA 19083, USA
E-mail: Uspen-and-sword@casematepublishers.com
Website: www.penandswordbooks.com

CONTENTS

INTRODUCTION

The last new station opened prior to 1 January 2018 – Forres, viewed on 24 March 2018.

Following the nationalisation of the railways in 1948, British Railways, through economic necessity and government policy, closed many of the branch lines and reduced the number of stations on the system until, by January 1978, there were just 2,358. On 1 January 2018 there were, according to National Rail, 2,560 operational stations on the system.* However this is not an altogether accurate figure as 2,580 would be closer to the mark. For accounting and operational purposes, a number of stations that were two or three individual ones are now considered as one. Typical examples are the former high and low level stations that originated with different companies such as at Lichfield, Tamworth, Glasgow Central, Glasgow Queen Street and Shotton.

* http://orr.gov.uk/__data/assets/pdf_file/0020/26129/estimates-of-station-usage-2016-17-key-facts.pdf

There are also a few anomalies. Heathrow Terminals 2 & 3, Heathrow Terminal 4 and Heathrow Terminal 5, although served by TOCs Heathrow Express and Heathrow Connect, are private stations on a private system so do not qualify for inclusion.

The demise of lines and stations from the 1960s onwards was blamed, amongst other things, on the explosion of car ownership and the irony is that one of the catalysts for the numerous station re-openings is precisely the same thing! There are so many vehicles choking the roads that large numbers are now turning to rail as a preferred method of travel!

Whilst councils and support groups actively pursued the reopening of branch lines and stations, it was an Act of Parliament in 1981 that provided the impetus. Tony Spellar, the MP for North Devon, proposed that BR could reopen lines and stations on a trial basis and close them if unsuccessful without having to go through the costly and time-consuming process for closure. This met with Parliamentary approval and the Transport Act 1962 (Amendment) 1981 came into effect on 2 August 1981 and changed the whole dynamics of station opening.

These openings can come within five categories.

a) Brand new on a new site (eg Imperial Wharf)
b) Reopening (eg Falls of Cruachan)
c) Reopenings on adjacent sites (eg Rutherglen)
d) Replacements (eg Rochester) and
e) Moving from non-timetabled or private to public stations (eg Allens West)

With regard to replacements, these have not added to the overall total as they encompass those stations that were opened immediately following the closure of another and usually retaining the same name.

There are some 26 that fall into this category with the replacements being made due to operational reasons, such as Bromsgrove (moved to a larger site to accommodate extra platforms and electrification) or Lochluichart (moved to a deviated line to accommodate a hydro-electric scheme) whilst the termini at Fort William, Wrexham Central and Windermere were moved to open up the original sites to commercial development. Others, such as Balloch and Uckfield, were moved and reopened to eliminate the need for a level crossing.

The purpose of this book is to record those that were opened or reopened in the seventy years between 1 January 1948 and 1 January 2018. Unless stated all photographs are by the authors.

Paul Smith and Sally Salmon
Birmingham 2018

KEY

X Appearing after the station name indicates that the station has ticket barriers

CATEGORIES

I	Number of platforms
A	Cash Machine
B	Shops
C	CSI (Customer Service Information) boards installed and/or public address announcements
D	Some disabled access to all platforms
D	Good disabled access to all platforms
H	Help Point and/or Pay Phone
P	Pay car park
P	Free car park
R	Refreshments available from vending machines or kiosk
R	Café with seating
S	Seating available
S	Seating available under cover
T	Ticket machines available
T	Ticket Office or Counter
W	Toilets available
X	Exit and Entrance numbers for 2016/17 as published by the Office of the Road & Rail Regulator
N/A	Indicates that the station was not open during 2016/17 or that the published figures include more than one station

ABBREVIATIONS

STATION MANAGING COMPANIES

AGA:	Abellio Greater Anglia
ASR:	Abellio ScotRail
ATW:	Arriva Trains Wales
ChR:	Chiltern Railway
EMT:	East Midlands Trains

GN:	Great Northern
GWR:	Great Western Railway
ILT:	Island Line Trains
LO:	London Overground
LU:	London Underground
M:	Merseyrail
NetR:	Network Rail
NR:	Northern Rail
SE:	Southeastern
So:	Southern
SR:	Stobart Rail
SWR:	South Western Railway
TL:	Thameslink
TP:	Trans Pennine
VTEC:	Virgin Trains East Coast
VT:	Virgin Trains
WMT:	West Midlands Trains

RAILWAY COMPANIES

CR:	Caledonian Railway
G&SWR:	Glasgow & South Western Railway
GNR:	Great Northern Railway
GWR:	Great Western Railway
HR:	Highland Railway
LB&SCR:	London, Brighton & South Coast Railway
LM&SR:	London Midland & Scottish Railway
L&NER:	London & North Eastern Railway
L&NWR:	London & North Western Railway
L&SWR:	London & South Western Railway
L&YR:	Lancashire & Yorkshire Railway
LPTE:	London Passenger Transport Executive
M&GN:	Midland & Great Northern Joint Line
MR:	Midland Railway
NBR:	North British Railway
NER:	North Eastern Railway
SE&CR:	South Eastern & Chatham Railway
SR:	Southern Railway

BRITISH RAILWAYS NEW AND REOPENED STATIONS 1948–2018

Stations closing and then reopening again within 6 months and temporary ones for events lasting just a few days are not included in this listing.

ABERCYNON NORTH

Location: ST 0828794885 (51.645254, -3.3268793)
Opened 3 October 1988 to allow the Aberdare line to serve Abercynon village, as the track layout in use at the time at the original station *(Abercynon South)* did not allow Aberdare services to call there. *Abercynon South* station was subsequently rebuilt to accommodate the Aberdare line and *Abercynon North* closed in May 2008. Upon closure of *Abercynon North*, *Abercynon South* was renamed as *Abercynon*

ABERDARE (ABA)

Looking north-east on 10 May 2015 with Class 150 Unit No.150279 waiting to depart to Cardiff Central.

Abernant Road, Aberdare, Mid-Glamorgan CF44 0NE
SO0047802744 (51.714563, -3.4419400)
Opened 3 October 1988.
ATW 1C**DHPST**T **569,364**

ACROW HALT

Location: TL5540038900 (52.026749, 0.26365284)
Opened 1 April 1957 to serve the adjacent Coronation Works of Acrow Engineering Ltd. It was closed, along with the branch to Saffron Walden, on 7 September 1964 but remained extant and heavily overgrown as recently as 2014.

ADWICK (AWK)

Church Lane, Adwick-le-Street, Doncaster,
South Yorkshire DN6 7AU
SE5440908682 (53.571925, -1.1798561)
Opened 11 October 1993.
NR 2C**DHP**R**SW** **197,926**

AIGBURTH (AIG)

Viewed on 10 Aug 2016.

Mersey Road, Liverpool L17 6AQ
SJ3841785707 (53.364625, -2.9269076)
Opened by the Garston and Liverpool Railway 1 June 1864 as *Mersey Road*, renamed as *Mersey Road and Aigburth* by the Cheshire Lines Committee in 1880, closed by BR 17 April 1972 and reopened 3 January 1978 as *Aigburth*.
M 2C**DHPSTW** **812,582**

AIRBLES (AIR)

Airbles Road, Airbles, North Lanarkshire ML1 2SX
NS7501456141 (55.782380, -3.9944911)
Opened 15 May 1989.
ASR 2**DHPS** **142,930**

ALFRETON (ALF)

Looking north on 20 May 2017.

Mansfield Road, Alfreton, Derbyshire DE55 7JQ
SK4229556161 (53.100978, -1.3697672)
Opened by the MR 1 May 1862, renamed as *Alfreton and South Normanton* 7 November 1891, closed 2 January 1967, reopened 7 May 1973 as *Alfreton and Mansfield Parkway* and reverted back to *Alfreton* 29 May 1994.
EMT 2CD**HPST**T**W 292,130**

ALLENS WEST (ALW)

Looking east on 24 September 2015 as Class 142 Unit No.142091 departs from Platform 2 on a service to Saltburn.

Durham Lane, Allens West, Stockton-on-Tees, Redcar and Cleveland TS16 0PF
NZ4147614572 (54.524746, -1.3607014)
Opened by the L&NER 4 October 1943 as *Urlay Nook Halt*, an unadvertised station to serve the nearby Royal Navy stores depot. Renamed as *Allens West Halt* 22 May 1944 and became a BR time-tabled station as *Allens West* 4 October 1971.
NR 2CD**HS 65,414**

ALLOA (ALO)

Station Road, Alloa, Clackmannanshire FK10 1BA
NS8889193122 (56.117870, -3.7885985)
Opened 15 May 2008.
This is sited to the east of the original station which was opened by the Stirling & Dunfermline Railway 28 August 1850, renamed as *Alloa North* by the NBR December 1875, renamed as *Alloa* January 1882 and closed by BR 7 October 1968.
ASR 1C**DHPST 360,596**

ALNESS (ASS)

Looking east on 16 September 2015 with the degraded former platform on the south side of the line in view on the right.

Station Road, Alness, Highland IV17 0SE
NH6598469413 (57.694504, -4.2525625)
Opened by Inverness & Ross-shire and Inverness & Aberdeen Junction Railways 23 March 1863, closed by BR 13 June 1960 and reopened 7 May 1973.
ASR 1**DHPS 26,376**

AMPRESS

Location: SZ31730 96950 (50.771272, -1.5513924)
Opened 1 October 1956 as *Ampress Works Halt* to serve the Welworthy Engineering Works. It was not in the public timetable and was renamed as *Ampress* by September 1970 and closed 6 October 1989. The platform was still extant in 2006.

ANDERSTON (AND) X

North Street, Anderston, Glasgow G3 8RR
NS5808565256 (55.859535, -4.2689616) (Subterranean)
Opened by Glasgow Central Railway 10 August 1896 as *Anderston Cross*, closed by BR 3 August 1959 and reopened 5 November 1979 as *Anderston*.
ASR 2C**HSTT 661,282**

APPERLEY BRIDGE (APY)

Looking west along Platform 2 on 18 June 2016 with the staggered Platform 1 in view in the distance.

Station Approach, Apperley Bridge, Bradford BD10 0FD
SE1959938409 (53.841564, -1.7036211)

Opened by the Leeds & Bradford Railway (leased to the MR) July 1846, renamed as *Apperley* in 1847, as *Apperley and Rawdon* 1 October 1890, as *Apperley Bridge and Rawdon* 20 December 1890 and as *Apperley Bridge* by BR 12 June 1961. It was closed 22 March 1965 and rebuilt and reopened 13 December 2015.
NR 2CD**PS**T **350,312**

ARDROSSAN HARBOUR (ADS)

Dock Road, Ardrossan Harbour, Ardrossan, North Ayrshire KA22 8DH
NS2257042073 (55.639727, -4.8206169)

Opened 15 September 1986.
ASR 1CD**HS** **121,004**

ARDROSSAN TOWN (ADN)

Princes Street, Ardrossan, North Ayrshire KA22 8DG
NS2309742087 (55.640048, -4.8122752)

Opened by the Ardrossan & Johnstone Railway in 1831 as *Ardrossan*, renamed as *Ardrossan Town* by BR 28 February 1953, closed 1 January 1968 and reopened 19 January 1987.
ASR 1CD**HS** **24,186**

ARGYLE STREET (AGS) **X**

35 Argyle Street, Glasgow G2 8AH
NS5922365010 (55.857660, -4.2506689) (Subterranean)

Opened 5 November 1979.
ASR 2BC**HS**TT **1,413,190**

ARLESEY (ARL)

Old Oak Close, Arlesey, Central Bedfordshire SG15 6XA
TL1903237772 (52.025601, -0.26652101)

Opened by the GNR 7 August 1850 as *Arlsey and Shefford Road*, renamed as *Arlesey and Shefford Road* in March 1860, as *Arlesey* in June 1893, as *Arlesey and Shefford Road* in July 1895, as *Arlesey and*

Henlow by the L&NER 1 March 1933, closed by BR 5 January 1959 and rebuilt and reopened 3 October 1988.
GN 2CD**HPS**TT **693,548**

ARMADALE (WEST LOTHIAN) (ARM)

Station Way, Armadale, West Lothian EH48 3BJ
NS94192 67218 (55.886441, -3.6931664)

Opened 4 March 2011.
ASR 2CD**HPS**T **238,688**

The original station, sited on the opposite side of the road bridge, was opened by the Bathgate & Coatbridge Railway 11 August 1862 and closed by BR 9 January 1956.

ARMATHWAITE (AWT)

Looking north on 31 May 2015.

Station Road, Armathwaite, Near Carlisle, Cumbria CA4 9PL
NY5047846352 (54.809574, -2.7720207)

Opened by the MR 1 May 1876, closed by BR 4 May 1970 and reopened 14 July 1986.

This station, as with those on this section of the Settle-Carlisle line, retains most of its original features, including buildings and lamp posts, kept in a delightfully restored condition.
NR 2**HPS** **2,180**

ASHCHURCH FOR TEWKESBURY (ASC)

Looking north on 8 March 2015.

Station Road, Ashchurch, Gloucestershire GL20 8TU
SO9263233392 (51.998916, -2.1087373)

Opened by the Birmingham and Gloucester Railway 24 June 1840 as *Ashchurch,* closed by BR 15 November 1971 and subsequently demolished, it was rebuilt and reopened 30 May 1997 as *Ashchurch for Tewkesbury.*
GWR 2C**DH**P**S** 94,244

ASHFIELD (ASF)

Viewed on 13 May 2017.

Ashfield Street, Ashfield, Glasgow G22 6SL
NS5947068475 (55.888839, -4.2485285)
Opened 3 December 1993.
ASR 2C**DHS** 50,340

ASHTON GATE HALT

Location: ST56704 71372 (51.439674, -2.6242974) (Approx)
Opened by the GWR 15 September 1906 as *Ashton Gate Platform,* closed August 1914, reopened 18 September 1920 for football use and 23 May 1926 for public use. Renamed as *Ashton Gate* in August 1928, as *Ashton Gate Halt* by BR 29 October 1962, closed 7 September 1964 and reopened for occasional use by football specials until 1974. It had two platforms primarily for football supporters travelling to the Ashton Gate ground of Bristol City FC.

AUCHINLECK (AUK)

Main Street, Auchinleck, Cumnock, East Ayrshire
KA18 2BH
NS5498021959 (55.469896, -4.2956442)
Opened by the Glasgow, Paisley, Kilmarnock and Ayr Railway 9 August 1848, closed by BR 6 December 1965 and reopened 14 May 1984.
ASR 2C**DH**P**S** 61,838

AYLESBURY VALE PARKWAY (AVP)

Bicester Road, Aylesbury, Buckinghamshire HP18 0PE
SP7869115308 (51.830852, -0.85946685)
Opened 14 December 2008.
ChR 1C**DH**P**RRS**TT**W** 169,164

Class 165 Unit No.165011 at the buffer stops on 7 September 2017.

BACHE (BAC)

Looking north on 17 May 2015.

Mill Lane, Chester CH2 1BS
SJ4056068283 (53.208269, -2.8914333)
Opened 9 January 1984.
M 2C**DHPS**T 360,100

BAGLAN (BAJ)

Looking south on 2 August 2015. This station is sandwiched between the M4 and the access road from Junction 41, which used to be part of the motorway before it was linked up to the western section in 1994.

Seaway Parade, Baglan, Port Talbot SA12 8ES
SS7481792164 (51.614346, -3.8093919)
Opened 2 June 1996.
ATW 2D**HPS** 23,776

BAILDON (BLD)

Viewed on 19 May 2016. As originally built the station had two platforms but at some point prior to reopening the track was singled.

Station Road, Baildon, Shipley, West Yorkshire BD17 6HS
SE1630739364 (53.850261, -1.7536128)
Opened by the MR 4 December 1876, closed by BR 5 January 1953, reopened 28 January 1957, closed 29 April 1957 and reopened 5 January 1973.
NR 1C**DPS** 289,944

BAILLIESTON (BIO)

Caledonia Road, Baillieston, Glasgow G69 7DQ
NS6776763285 (55.844591, -4.1134364)
Opened 4 October 1993.
ASR 2CD**HS** 56,480

BALLIFURTH FARM HALT

Location: NJ0140923599 (57.292315, -3.6374912)
One of four halts opened on the Speyside route between Elgin and Aviemore on 15 June 1959, on the introduction of railbuses, and closed by the British Railways Board on 18 October 1965 when services on the line were withdrawn.

BALLOCH (BHC)

Balloch Road, Alexandria, West Dunbartonshire G83 8SS
NS3901081841 (56.002410, -4.5832974)
Opened 24 April 1988 as *Balloch Central* and renamed 15 May 1989 as *Balloch*. This station replaced *Balloch* which was opened 15 July 1850 by the Caledonian and Dumbartonshire Junction Railway, renamed by BR 30 June 1952 as *Balloch Central* and closed 24 April 1988 to eliminate a level crossing.
ASR 1C**DHSTW** 543,006

BALMOSSIE (BSI)

South Balmossie Street, Balmossie, Dundee DD5 4QH
NO4843531705 (56.474631, -2.8386575)
Opened 18 June 1962 as *Balmossie Halt* and re-named as *Balmossie* 16 May 1983.
ASR 2CD**HS** 1,364

BALNACRA LEVEL CROSSING GATEHOUSE

Location: NG98417 46477 (57.463646, -5.3626250)
Opened 3 December 1951 and closed after 1984.

BARGEDDIE (BGI)

Longmuir Road, Bargeddie, Glasgow G69 7TS
NS7027263956 (55.851300, -4.0737772)
Opened 4 October 1993.
ASR 2CD**HPS** 114,912

BARROW-UPON-SOAR (BWS)

Class 156 Unit No.156404 departing northbound on 15 August 2015.

Grove Lane, Barrow-on-Soar, Loughborough, Leicestershire LE12 8US
SK5778217209 (52.749418, -1.1454004)
Opened 30 May 1994.
EMT 2**HS** 87,792

BASILDON (BSO) X

Looking west on 12 July 2015.

Station Way, Basildon, Essex SS16 5XY
TQ7036988340 (51.568195, 0.45680988)
Opened 25 November 1974.
c2c 2**ABCDHRSTTW** 3,180,178

BATHGATE (1ST BR)

Location: NS97450 68550 (55.899108, -3.6416165)
The station opened 24 March 1986 when the rail service from Edinburgh was re-introduced by British Rail. It was sited on the location of the original Bathgate station, which became the town's goods station when Bathgate Upper opened, and closed on 10 October 2010 when the current station opened.

BATHGATE (BHG) X

Edinburgh Road, Bathgate, West Lothian EH48 1BA
NS9777168325 (55.897156, -3.6363948)
Opened 10 October 2010. This station replaced one sited some 750 yards to the east (See Bathgate [1st BR]).
ASR 2C**DH**PST**TW** 1,302,786

BEASDALE (BSL)

A830, South of Druimindarroch, Beasdale, Highland PH39 4NR
NM7089885058 (56.900074, -5.7638854)
Opened by the NBR 1 April 1901 as a private station for Arisaig House, but was also available for public use. It was officially opened as a public station by BR 6 September 1965.
ASR 1**HS** 312

BEAULY (BEL)

Station Road, Beauly, Highland IV4 7EF
NH5201345798 (57.478200, -4.4697327)
Opened by the Inverness & Ross-shire Railway 11 June 1862, closed by BR 13 June 1960, and reopened 15 April 2002. The station platform, measuring only 49.4ft in length, is the shortest in Britain.
ASR 1C**DH**PS 52,870

BEDFORD (BDM) X

Ashburnham Road, Bedford MK40 1DS
TL0417649679 (52.135602, -0.47933346)
Opened 9 October 1978 as *Bedford Midland* and renamed as *Bedford* 16 May 1988. This station was built as a replacement for *Bedford Midland Road* which was sited about 110 yards to the south and is now occupied by a car park.
TL 5**AB**C**DH**P**RS**TT**W** 3,941,363

BEDFORD ST JOHNS (BSJ)

Looking south on 3 July 2016. This replaced *Bedford* station which was opened by the L&NWR 1 August 1862, renamed as *Bedford St Johns* by the LM&SR 2 June 1924 and closed by BR 14 May 1984.

Melbourne Street, Bedford MK42 9AN
TL0498349007 (52.129411, -0.46840155)
Opened 14 May 1984 as *Bedford St Johns Halt* and subsequently renamed as *Bedford St Johns*.
WMT 1**HPS** 183,826

BEDWORTH (BEH)

Looking north along Platform 2 on 24 December 2015.

Bulkington Road, Bedworth, Nuneaton, Warwickshire CV12 8JF
SP3626186963 (52.479399, -1.4675230)
Opened by the L&NWR 2 September 1850, closed by BR 18 January 1965 and reopened 16 May 1988.
WMT 2C**DHS** 85,310

BELLE VUE (BLV)

Viewed on 19 May 2016, this station replaced the original one opened by the Sheffield and Midland Railway Companies' Committee 1 September 1875 and closed by BR 27 March 1986.

Glencastle Road, Off Hyde Road,
Gorton, Manchester M18 7BN
SJ8813296133 (53.461811, -2.1802235)
Opened 27 March 1986.
NR 2**HS** 11,456

BENTLEY (SOUTH YORKS) (BYK)

Looking north on 16 April 2016. A previous station on this site was a wooden halt known as *Bentley Crossing* which was opened by the West Riding and Grimsby Railway in February 1914 and closed by the L&NER in 1943.

Church Street, Bentley, Doncaster, South Yorkshire DN5 0BE
SE5636605581 (53.543855, -1.1508560)
Opened 27 April 1992.
NR 2DP**S** 130,434

BERMUDA PARK (BEP)

Looking north on 28 April 2016.

St Georges Way, Bermuda Industrial Estate, Nuneaton,
Warwickshire CV10 7JS
SP3589489644 (52.503524, -1.4726374)
Opened 18 January 2016.
WMT 2C**DHS**T 20,106

BERRY BROW (BBW)

Birch Road, Berry Brow, Huddersfield, West Yorkshire
HD4 7LP
SE1375513855 (53.621060, -1.7935291)

Looking north on 18 June 2016. The first *Berry Brow* station was sited 330 yards to the north and was opened by the Huddersfield and Sheffield Junction Railway 1 July 1850, closed by BR 4 July 1966 and subsequently demolished.

Opened 9 October 1989.
NR 1D**S** 30,316

BICESTER VILLAGE (BIT) **X**

Looking north on 27 December 2015.

London Road, Bicester OX26 6HU
SP5868721965 (51.893156, -1.1485923)
Opened by the Buckinghamshire Railway 1 October 1850 as *Bicester*, renamed as *Bicester London Road* by BR March 1954, closed 1 January 1968 and reopened 11 May 1987 as *Bicester Town*. It was closed again 15 February 2014 to accommodate rebuilding and reopened as *Bicester Village* 25 October 2015.
ChR 2C**DHPRSTW** 1,311,238

BILLINGHAM (CLEVELAND) (BIL)

Marsh House Avenue, Billingham, Cleveland TS23 3TG
NZ4662823631 (54.605706, -1.2796665)

Viewed on 25 September 2015. This station replaced *Billingham-on-Tees* which was sited 900 yards to the south-west and opened in January 1836 by the Clarence Railway.

Opened 7 November 1966.
NR 2C**HPS** 94,994

BIRCHWOOD (BWD)

Looking east on 10 August 2016.

Dewhurst Road, Birchwood, Warrington WA3 7PU
SJ6512790768 (53.412560, -2.5261051)
Opened 6 October 1980.
NR 2B CDR**STTW** 712,562

BIRMINGHAM INTERNATIONAL (BHI) **X**

Stationlink Road, Bickenhill Lane, Solihull,
West Midlands B40 1PA
SP1877283676 (52.450727, -1.7252088)
Opened 26 January 1976.
VT 5**ABC**DHPR**RSTTW** 6,468,034

Looking west on 17 August 2015, Birmingham Airport is on the left and the NEC on the right.

BIRMINGHAM MOOR STREET (BMO) **X**

Ex-GWR Class 4900 Hall 4-6-0 No.4965 *Rood Ashton Hall* passing through the station on 31 July 2016 with empty stock for the *Shakespeare Express*.

Queensway, Birmingham B4 7UL
Location: SP07421 86744 (52.478573, -1.8921636)
Opened by the GWR 1 July 1909, it was originally built as a terminus but was closed by BR May 1967 and reopened 8 May 1978. Two new platforms were constructed on the adjacent main line 26 September 1987 and the terminus portion was again closed. A restoration project was undertaken during the 1990s and the original station was connected to the new platforms and reopened 11 December 2010.
ChR 4**ABC**DH**RRSTTW** 6,803,086

BIRMINGHAM SNOW HILL (BSW) **X**

Colmore Row, Birmingham B3 2BJ
SP0686287384 (52.484335, -1.9003779)
Opened by the GWR 1 October 1852 as *Birmingham*, renamed as *Birmingham Snow Hill* February 1858 and closed by BR

Looking south on 28 August 2015 with Class 172 Unit No.172218 standing on Platform 3. This station also accommodated the Midland Metro until 24 October 2015 when the tramway was diverted around the station and extended to Birmingham New Street.

6 March 1972 and subsequently demolished. It was rebuilt and reopened 5 October 1987.
WMT 3B**CDH**PR**ST**T**W** 4,450,874

BLACKHORSE ROAD (BHO) **X**

Looking east on 22 August 2017. This replaced the original *Black Horse Road* station which was opened by the Tottenham and Forest Gate Joint Railway 9 July 1894 and sited on the opposite side of the road bridge. The new station was built to provide a better interchange with the Victoria Line Tube Station which had opened on 1 September 1968.

Blackhorse Road, Walthamstow, Greater London E17 6NH
TQ3579889348 (51.586633, -0.041269094)
Opened 14 December 1981.
LU 2B**CH**P**ST** 774,220

BLACKPOOL PLEASURE BEACH (BPB)

Burlington Road, Blackpool, Lancashire FY4 1NY
SD3066532912 (53.787887, -3.0538673)
Opened 13 April 1987.
NR 1D**HS** 105,466

Looking north on 8 April 2017. This is built on the site of *Burlington Road* station which was opened by the Preston and Wyre Joint Railway 1 October 1913, closed 1 October 1915, reopened by August 1919 and closed by the LM&SR 11 September 1939.

BLACKRIDGE (BKR)

Westrigg Way, Blackridge, West Lothian EH48 3BW
NS90634 67084 (55.884440, -3.7499702)
Opened 12 December 2010. An earlier station, *Westcraigs*, was sited some 660 yards to the west and had been opened by the Bathgate & Coatbridge Railway 11 August 1862 and closed by BR 9 January 1956.
ASR 2**CDH**P**ST** 56,894

BLAENAU FFESTINIOG (BFF)

Looking west on 16 July 2015 with the platforms for the 1ft 11.5in narrow gauge of the Ffestiniog Railway in view on the left and the 4ft 8.5in standard gauge on the right.

Church Street, Blaenau Ffestiniog, Gwynedd LL41 3HE
SH7000145903 (52.994634, -3.9383525)
Opened jointly by BR and the Ffestiniog Railway 21 March 1982 as *Blaenau Ffestiniog Central* and subsequently renamed as *Blaenau Ffestiniog*. Platform 1 (standard gauge) is operated by ATW and Platforms 2 & 3 (narrow gauge) by the Ffestiniog Railway.
ATW & **Ffestiniog Railway** 3**CDH**P**S** 40,710

BLAYDON (BLO)
Tyne Street, Blaydon on Tyne NE21 4JB
NZ1846263524 (54.966003, -1.7131704)
Opened by the Newcastle and Carlisle Railway 9 March 1835, closed by BR 3 September 1966 and reopened 1 May 1967.
NR 2**S** 15,128

BLENCOW
Location: NY4638030416 (54.665958, -2.8328405) (Approx)
Opened by the Cockermouth, Keswick & Penrith Railway 2 January 1865, closed by BR 3 March 1952, reopened 2 July 1956 and closed 6 March 1972.

BLOXWICH (BLX)

Looking along Platform 1 on 22 July 2015. This station replaced an earlier one that was opened by the South Staffordshire Railway 1 February 1858 and closed by BR 18 January 1965. It was sited about 250 yards south of the current station.

Croxdene Avenue, Bloxwich, Walsall, West Midlands WS3 2NY
SJ9930602296 (52.618432, -2.0116842)
Opened 17 April 1989.
WMT 2CD**H**S**T** 49,672

BLOXWICH NORTH (BWN)

Looking along Platform 2 on 22 July 2015.

Broad Lane, Bloxwich, Walsall, West Midlands WS3 2TZ
SJ9891703046 (52.625177, -2.0174349)
Opened 2 October 1990. It was planned to open as *Broad Lane* but was renamed as *Bloxwich North* prior to opening.
WMT 2CD**HPS**T 51,300

BOLSOVER CASTLE
Location: SK4625070650 (53.230882, -1.3086089)
Opened by MR 1 September 1880 as *Bolsover*, closed by the LM&SR 28 July 1930, but used for excursions until 1939. Reopened by BR 28 July 1977 as *Bolsover Castle* for summer excursions and closed in 1981.

BOOTHFERRY PARK HALT
Location: TA0635828404 (53.741181, -0.38888946)
Opened 6 January 1951 and closed in 1986.

BOSCARNE EXCHANGE PLATFORM
Location: SX0409467447 (50.474024, -4.7622795) (Approx)
Opened 15 June 1964, closed 18 April 1966, reopened 2 May 1966 and closed 30 January 1967.

BRADFORD FORSTER SQUARE (BDQ) X

Looking south towards the buffer stops on 18 June 2016. This was built on the west side of the original station which was opened by the MR 2 March 1890 as *Bradford* and renamed as *Bradford Forster Square* by the LM&SR 2 June 1924. It closed on the day that the new one opened and was subsequently demolished.

St Blaise Way, Bradford BD1 4QQ
SE1637533444 (53.797045, -1.7528886)
Opened 11 June 1990.
NR 3**AB**CD**H**PR**ST**T 2,112,894

BRADFORD INTERCHANGE (BDI) X
Bridge Street, Bradford BD1 1TU
SE1661932719 (53.790527, -1.7492193)
Opened 14 January 1973 as *Bradford Exchange* and renamed as *Bradford Interchange* 16 May 1983. The original station was sited about 160 yards to the north and was opened by the Manchester and Leeds Railway 5 May 1850 as *Bradford Drake Street* and renamed as *Bradford Exchange* by the L&YR in 1890.
NR 4**AB**CD**H**S**TT**W 2,976,052

BRAINTREE FREEPORT (BTP)

Looking north on 20 August 2017.

Charter Way, Chapel Hill Retail Park, Braintree,
Essex CM77 8YH
TL7691522078 (51.869218, 0.56827900)
Opened 8 November 1999.
AGA 1CD**HS**T **82,698**

BRAMLEY (W. YORKS) (BLE)

Looking along Platform 2 on 18 June 2016 with the staggered Platform 1 in view in the distance.

Swinnow Road, Bramley, Leeds LS13 4DN
SE2395234419 (53.805517, -1.6377795)
Opened by the Leeds, Bradford and Halifax Junction Railway 1 August 1854, closed by BR 4 July 1966 and reopened 12 September 1983.
NR 2C**HPS** **345,974**

BRANCHTON (BCN)

Inverkip Road, Branchton, Greenock,
Inverclyde PA16 0XR
NS2496375487 (55.940464, -4.8041380)
Opened 5 June 1967. This replaced *Upper Greenock* station which was sited about 1.2 miles east and was opened by the Glasgow and Wemyss Bay Railway 15 May 1865.
ASR 1CD**HPS** **113,200**

BRIDGE OF ALLAN (BEA)

Station Road, Bridge of Allan, Stirling FK9 4PH
NS7852497698 (56.156432, -3.9573110)
Opened 13 May 1985. This station replaced the original one that was sited a few hundred yards to the north and was opened by the Scottish Central Railway 1 June 1848 and closed by BR 1 November 1965.
ASR 2CD**HPS**T **271,416**

BRIDGETON (BDG)

1 Bridgeton Cross, Bridgeton, Glasgow G40 1BN
NS6078663945 (55.848557, -4.2251772)
Opened by the Glasgow Central Railway 1 November 1895 as *Bridgeton Cross*, closed by BR 5 October 1964 and reopened 5 November 1979 as *Bridgeton*.
ASR 2C**HST** **610,466**

BRIGHOUSE (BGH)

Looking along Platform 2 on 18 June 2016. The first station here was sited about 300 yards to the east and was opened by the Manchester and Leeds Railway 5 October 1840 as *Brighouse for Rastrick*. It closed 1 May 1893.

Railway Street, Brighouse, West Yorkshire HD6 1LE
SE1468122432 (53.698126, -1.7791152)
Opened by the L&YR 1 May 1893 as *Brighouse for Rastrick*, closed by BR 5 January 1970 and reopened 28 May 2000 as *Brighouse*.
NR 2CD**HPS** **427,758**

BRINNINGTON (BNT)

Looking south-east along Platform 1 on 24 October 2015.

The Link, Middlesex Road, Brinnington,
Stockport SK5 8JE
SJ9114792833 (53.432204, -2.1347064)
Opened 12 December 1997.
NR 2CD**ST** **79,512**

BRISTOL PARKWAY (BPW) X
Stoke Gifford, Bristol BS34 8PU
ST6249879581 (51.513897, -2.5418175)
Opened 1 May 1972.
GWR 4**AB**CDHPRST**TW** **2,499,246**

BRITON FERRY (BNF)

Looking north along Platform 2 on 2 August 2015. This station replaced
Briton Ferry which was opened by the GWR 16 September 1935 and
closed by BR 2 November 1964.

Rockingham Terrace, Briton Ferry, Neath SA11 2NE
SS7414494783 (51.637727, -3.8200617)
Opened 1 June 1994.
ATW 2CD**HPS** **36,900**

BROMBOROUGH RAKE (BMR)

Viewed on 17 May 2015.

The Rake, Bromborough, Wirral CH62 7AL
SJ3415181935 (53.330216, -2.9902077)
Opened 30 September 1985.
M 2C**HST** **271,634**

BROMSGROVE (BMV)

Viewed on 14 July 2016, two days after its official opening, this station
replaced the original one which was sited 350 yards to the north and
was opened by the Birmingham and Gloucester Railway 24 June 1840.
It was situated at the foot of the 2 mile long 1 in 37.7 gradient Lickey
Incline and in steam days there was a shed here to provide and service
a fleet of banking locomotives.

New Road, Aston Fields, Bromsgrove, Worcestershire B60 3SB
SO9671169153 (52.320471, -2.04967710)
Opened 12 July 2016.
WMT 4CD**HPST**T**W** **644,350**

BRUNSTANE (BSU)
Brunstane Road South, Brunstane, Edinburgh EH15 2NG
NT3133172699 (55.942414, -3.1009615)
Opened 3 June 2002.
ASR 1CD**HST** **162,074**

BRUNSWICK (BRW)

Viewed on 10 August 2016.

Sefton Street, Liverpool L8 6XP
SJ3517887822 (53.383252, -2.9760081)
Opened 9 March 1998.
M 2CD**HP**RST **1,037,186**

BUCKSHAW PARKWAY (BSV)

Looking along Platform 1 on 26 April 2016, it is built on the site of *Chorley ROF Platform* which was opened by the LM&SR 7 February 1938, renamed as *Chorley Halt* prior to May 1942 and closed by BR c1963.

Station Approach, Buckshaw Village, Chorley PR7 7EY
SD5653619818 (53.673013, -2.6593894)
Opened 3 October 2011.
NR 2C**DHPS**TT**W** 353,688

BULWELL (BLW)

Looking south on 3 May 2015. The Nottingham Express Transit tram line was opened in March 2004 and this utilised the northbound track with the tram stop, in view on the right, now occupying the site of the former northbound station platform.

Station Road, Bulwell, Nottinghamshire NG6 9AA
SK5409044965 (52.999286, -1.1954880)
Opened by the MR 2 October 1848, renamed as *Bulwell Market* by BR 11 August 1952, closed 12 October 1964 and reopened as *Bulwell* 23 May 1994.
EMT 1C**DHPS** 59,632

BURLEY PARK (BUY)

Viewed on 21 May 2017.

Ashville Road, Leeds LS6 1NA
SE2788835182 (53.812185, -1.5779549)
Opened 28 November 1998.
NR 2C**DPS** 739,308

BURNLEY MANCHESTER ROAD (BYM)

Looking north along Platform 2 on 28 June 2015.

Manchester Road, Burnley BB11 4HU
SD8365432145 (53.785365, -2.2495747)
Opened by the L&YR 1 November 1866, closed by BR 6 November 1961 and rebuilt and reopened 29 September 1986.
NR 2C**DHPS**TT 433,396

BUTLERS LANE (BUL)

Butlers Lane, Four Oaks, Sutton Coldfield, Birmingham B74 4RT
SP1102499477 (52.592979, -1.8386978)

Looking north along Platform 2 on 7 June 2015.

Looking north along Platform 1 on 29 August 2015. This station was closed between 21 October 1991 and 23 March 1992 for major refurbishment prior to the introduction of electrified services.

Opened 30 September 1957 as *Butlers Lane Halt* and renamed April 1963 as *Butlers Lane*.
WMT 2C**HS**T**T** 229,830

CAISTER CAMP HALT
Location: TG5225013449 (52.660027, 1.7286532)
Opened by the M&GN 17 July 1933, closed September 1939, reopened June 1948 and closed 27 September 1958 (last train) – officially 2 March 1959.

CALDERCRUIX (CAC)
Millstream Crescent, Caldercruix, Airdrie, North Lanarkshire ML6 7UL
NS8200567705 (55.887978, -3.8881147)
Opened by the Bathgate and Coatbridge Railway 11 August 1862, closed by BR 9 January 1956 and reopened 13 February 2011.
ASR 2C**DHPS**T 88,688

CALDERPARK HALT FOR THE ZOO
Location: West of Baillieston NS6821662195 (55.834928, -4.1057432) (Approx)
Opened 5 July 1951 and closed 4 July 1955.

CALIFORNIA HALT
Location: TG5145014749 (52.672060, 1.7178414)
Opened by the M&GN 17 July 1933, closed September 1939, reopened June 1948 and closed 27 September 1958 (last train) – officially 2 March 1959.

CAM & DURSLEY (CDU)
Station Approach, Off Box Road,
Gloucestershire GL11 5DJ
SO7527102160 (51.717617, -2.3593629)
Opened 29 May 1994.
GWR 2C**DHPS**T 201,188

CAMBRIDGE NORTH (CMB) X

Viewed on 12 July 2017.

Cowley Road, Cambridge CB4 0WZ
Location: TL 47507 60560 (52.223501, 0.15808403)
Opened 21 May 2017.
AGA 3C**DH**PS**STW,N/A**

CAMELON (CMO)
8-88 Glasgow Road (Mariner Leisure Centre),
Falkirk FK1 4DD
NS8671580750 (56.006258, -3.8183311)
Opened 25 September 1994.
ASR 2C**DHPS**T 132,166

CANADA WATER (ZCW)
Surrey Quays Road, Surrey Quays, London SE16 7EF
TQ3547479480 (51.498034, -0.049730837) (Subterranean)
Opened 19 August 1999.
LU 2AB**CDHRS**T 25,015,768

CANNOCK (CAO)

Girton Road, Cannock, Staffordshire WS11 0EG
SJ9859009841 (52.686259, -2.0222917)
Opened by the South Staffordshire Railway 1 February 1858, closed by BR 18 January 1965 and rebuilt and reopened 10 April 1989.
WMT 2CD**HPS**T **233,172**

CARFIN (CRF)

Newarthill Road, Carfin, South Lanarkshire ML1 5AX
NS7754958876 (55.807588, -3.9553168)
Opened by the LM&SR 1 October 1927 as *Carfin Halt*, closed and then reopened by BR and subsequently renamed as *Carfin* 16 May 1983.
ASR 2CD**HPS 131,190**

CARMYLE (CML)

Carmyle Avenue, Carmyle, Glasgow G32 8JU
NS6493462223 (55.834274, -4.1581187)
Opened by the Rutherglen and Coatbridge Railway 8 January 1866, and worked from the outset by the CR, it was closed by BR 5 October 1964 and reopened 4 October 1993.
ASR 2CD**HS 155,484**

CARPENDERS PARK (CPK) X

Looking north on 26 May 2016. This station replaced an earlier one that was sited 230 yards to the north and opened by the L&NWR 1 April 1914 as *Carpenders Park*, closed 1 January 1917, reopened 5 May 1919 and closed by BR 17 November 1952.

Prestwick Road, Watford, Hertfordshire WD19 7DT
TQ1183693388 (51.628204, -0.38568288)
Opened 17 November 1952.
LO 2CD**HRS**TT **1,189,056**

CATHAYS (CYS) X

Park Place, Cardiff CF10 3AT
ST1825577311 (51.488817, -3.1787530)
Opened 3 October 1983.
ATW 2CH**S**TT **954,372**

Looking south along Platform 2 on 24 May 2015.

CHAFFORD HUNDRED LAKESIDE (CFH) X

Looking south on 26 February 2017.

Fleming Road, Chafford Hundred, Grays, Essex RM16 6QQ
TQ5892478793 (51.485764, 0.28751537)
Opened 30 May 1995 as *Chafford Hundred* and renamed as *Chafford Hundred Lakeside* in January 2013.
c2c 1C**DH**PR**STTW 3,883,758**

CHANDLERS FORD (CFR)

Looking north on 3 October 2015. Between closure and reopening the track had been singled which meant that the southbound platform, in view on the right, was redundant and when the station was formally reopened 19 October 2003 only the original northbound platform was utilized.

Station Lane, Chandlers Ford, Eastleigh SO53 4DE
SU4327420633 (50.983480, -1.3848983)
Opened by the L&SWR in February 1848, closed by BR 5 May 1969 and reopened 18 May 2003.
SWR 1C**DHPS**T**T 230,174**

CHAPELTOWN (SOUTH YORKS) (CLN)

Class 144 Unit No.144018 on Platform 1 on 7 May 2016. This station replaced *Chapeltown* which was sited just to the north and opened by the MR 1 July 1897. This was renamed as *Chapeltown South* by BR 18 June 1951, reverted back to *Chapeltown* 20 February 1969 and closed 2 August 1982.

Market Place, Chapeltown, Sheffield S35 2UU
SK3552696318 (53.462414, -1.4663771)
Opened 2 August 1982.
NR 2C**DHS**T **343,278**

CHATELHERAULT (CTE)

Leven Road, Hamilton, South Lanarkshire ML3 7WS
NS7433454247 (55.765191, -4.0044482)
Opened by the Lesmahagow Railway 1 December 1866 as *Ferniegair*, it was rebuilt and reopened by the CR 2 October 1876, closed 1 January 1917 and rebuilt again and reopened by BR 12 December 2005 as *Chatelherault.*
ASR 1C**DHPS 105,464**

CHELLASTON

Location: SK3755330047 (52.866600, -1.4436049)
Opened by the MR 1 September 1868, renamed as *Chellaston and Swarkestone* 15 June 1901, closed by the LM&SR 22 September 1930, reopened by BR for excursion traffic as *Chellaston* prior to 17 May 1959 and closed after August 1962.

CHELTENHAM RACECOURSE

Location: SO9547625119 (51.924572, -2.0671973)
Opened by the GWR 13 March 1912, closed by BR 25 March 1968, reopened 16 March 1971 and closed 18 March 1976. Reopened as part of the Gloucester Warwickshire Railway heritage line prior to 7 April 2003.

CHESTERTON LANE HALT

Location: SP02418 01080 (51.708452, -1.9664057)
Opened 2 February 1959 and closed 6 April 1964.

CHURCH'S HILL HALT

Location: ST93200 96300 (51.665436, -2.0997163)
Opened 2 February 1959 and closed 6 April 1964.

CITY THAMESLINK (CTK) X

Ludgate Hill, Greater London EC4M 7JH
TQ3168081154 (51.513973, -0.10373210) (Subterranean)
Opened 29 May 1990 as *St Paul's Thameslink* and renamed as *City Thameslink* 30 September 1991.
TL 2**ABCDHRS**T**TW 6,339,202**

CLITHEROE (CLH)

Viewed on 31 May 2015, this station replaced an earlier one, sited about 220 yards to the south, which was opened by the Bolton, Blackburn, Clitheroe and West Yorkshire Railway 22 June 1850 and closed by the L&YR in 1893/4. As can be seen, the platforms on the current station are slightly staggered.

Station Road, Clitheroe, Lancashire BB7 2ED
SD7416742017 (53.873703, -2.3943812)
Opened by the L&YR in 1893/4, totally closed by BR 10 September 1962 and used for excursion and summer weekend traffic until fully reopened 29 May 1994.
NR 2C**DHS**T**W 284,362**

COLESHILL PARKWAY (CEH)

Station Road, Birmingham B46 1JZ
SP1993890999 (52.516516, -1.7076203)
Opened 19 August 2007.
WMT 2C**DHPS**T**T 286,992**

Looking west along Platform 2 on 21 June 2015. This is built on the site of *Forge Mills* station which was opened by the Birmingham & Derby Junction Railway 10 February 1842, renamed as *Forge Mills for Coleshill* 1 November 1849, as *Forge Mills* by the MR 1 April 1904 and as *Coleshill* by the LM&SR 9 July 1923. It was closed by BR 4 March 1968.

COLNBROOKE ESTATE HALT
Location: TQ03925 77286 (51.484984, -0.50467908)
Opened 1 May 1961 and closed 29 March 1965.

CONON BRIDGE (CBD)
Station Road, Conon Bridge, Dingwall, Highland IV7 8AA
NH5410355023 (57.561666, -4.4404346)
Opened by the Inverness & Ross-shire Railway 11 June 1862 as *Conon*, closed by BR 13 June 1960 and rebuilt and reopened 8 February 2013 as *Conon Bridge*. The original station had two platforms and was the proposed junction for the Cromarty and Dingwall Light Railway. Construction for this commenced in c1902 and ceased at the outbreak of the First World War when the six miles of track that had been completed was lifted for use elsewhere.
ASR 1C**DHPS** 15,494

CONONLEY (CEY)

Viewed on 19 May 2016.

Cononley Road, Cononley, Keighley, West Yorkshire BD20 8LS
SD99313 46801 (53.917357, -2.0119518)
Opened by the Leeds and Bradford Extension Railway in December 1847, closed by BR 22 March 1965 and reopened 20 April 1988.
NR 2CD**HPS** 177,918

CONWAY PARK (CNP) **X**

Looking north-west along Platform 2 on 17 May 2015. The station is below ground level and the line was originally in a tunnel. This tunnel was excavated, the roof opened out and the track bed widened to accommodate the platforms and station buildings.

Europa Boulevard, Birkenhead CH41 4PP
SJ3208289000 (53.393444, -3.0227912) (Semi-subterranean)
Opened 22 June 1998.
M 2CD**H**R**STW** 897,220

CONWY (CNW)

Looking north along Platform 1 on 19 July 2015.

Rosemary Lane, Conwy LL32 8LD
SH7803577470 (53.280130, -3.8307423)
Opened by the Chester & Holyhead Railway 1 May 1848 as *Conway*, closed by BR 14 February 1966 and reopened 29 June 1987 as *Conwy*.
ATW 2CD**HPS** 48,832

CORBY (COR)

Looking north on 10 September 2015. Visible on the left hand side is one of the platforms of the original station here which was opened by the MR 1 March 1880 as *Corby and Cottingham* and closed by BR on 4 June 1990.

Station Road, Corby, Northamptonshire NN17 1UJ
SP8915388675 (52.488713, -0.68844661)
Opened 23 February 2009.
EMT 1C**DH**PS**TTW** 272,162

CORKERHILL (CKH)

281 Corkerhill Road, Corkerhill, Glasgow G52 1QR
NS5392162925 (55.837364, -4.3341681)
Opened by the G&SWR 1 December 1896 as *Corkerhill Halt*, renamed as *Corkerhill* by the LM&SR in 1933/4, closed by BR 10 January 1983 and reopened 30 July 1990.
ASR 1C**DHS** 284,918

COTTINGLEY (COT)

Looking along Platform 2 on 17 May 2016.

Cottingley Drive, Leeds, West Yorkshire LS11 0JT
SE2728330240 (53.767800, -1.5875754)
Opened 25 April 1988.
NR 2C**HS** 97,180

COVENTRY ARENA (CAA)

Class 153 Unit No.153365 on a service to Nuneaton on 28 April 2016. Although built to serve the adjacent arena it was decided that the station would not be open on match days as it would not be capable of handling a large number of people over a short space of time and the only timetabled service was diagrammed to a single Class 153 unit.

Arena Park Shopping Centre, Classic Drive,
Coventry CV6 6AS
SP3445083370 (52.447209, -1.4945564)
Opened 18 January 2016.
WMT 2C**DH**PST 86,706

CRAIG HOUSES

Location: NH04029 49211(57.490619, -5.2714237) (Approx)
Opened 3 December 1951 and closed after May 1972.

CRANBROOK (DEVON) (CBK)

Looking west on 25 May 2017.

Burrough Fields, Cranbrook, Exeter, Devon EX5 2DY
SX99847 95455 (50.750030, -3.4210315)
Opened 13 December 2015.
SWR 1C**DH**PST 90,458

CRAWLEY (CRW) **X**

Looking along Platform 1 on 24 June 2017. This station replaced the original one, sited immediately west and opened by the LB&SCR 14 February 1848.

Station Way, Crawley, West Sussex RH10 1JA
TQ2702436317 (51.112077, -0.18674880)
Opened 28 July 1968.
So 2C**DPRST**TW **1,652,874**

CRESSINGTON (CSG)

Viewed on 10 August 2016.

Knowsley Road, Cressington, Liverpool L19 0PE
SJ3940385035 (53.358700, -2.9119590)
Opened by the Garston and Liverpool Railway 1 March 1873 as *Cressington*, renamed as *Cressington and Grassendale* by the Cheshire Lines Committee in April 1877, closed by BR 17 April 1972 and reopened as *Cressington* 3 January 1978.
M 2C**HPRST** **490,986**

CRESWELL (CWD)

Station Road, Creswell, Derbyshire S80 4HB
SK5236274406 (53.264074, -1.2164435)

Looking north along Platform 2 towards the signal box on 3 May 2015.

Opened by the MR 1 June 1875, renamed as *Elmton and Cresswell* 10 April 1886, as *Elmton and Creswell* 1 May 1887, closed by BR 12 October 1964 and rebuilt and reopened 25 May 1998 as *Creswell*.
EMT 2C**DP**S **43,434**

CROOKSTON (CKT)

Crookston Road, Glasgow G52 3TX
NS5200863538 (55.842284, -4.3650189)
Opened by the G&SWR 1 July 1885, closed 1 January 1917, reopened 10 February 1919, closed by BR 10 January 1983 and reopened 30 July 1990.
ASR 1C**DHS**T **188,064**

CROSSFLATTS (CFL)

Viewed on 19 May 2016.

Keighley Road, Crossflatts, Bingley, West Yorkshire BD16 2RZ
SE1031540254 (53.858409, -1.8446544)
Opened 17 May 1982.
NR 2C**DPS**T **544,516**

CROSSKEYS (CKY)

Looking north-west along Platform 2 on 24 May 2015. This replaced *Cross Keys* station which was opened by the Monmouthshire Railway 21 December 1850, closed by BR 30 April 1962 and was sited nearby.

Off Risca Road, Crosskeys, Caerphilly NP11 7BU
ST2214491938 (51.620854, -3.1259993)
Opened 7 June 2008.
ATW 2CD**HS**T **118,604**

CULKERTON

Location: ST9317796295 (51.665395, -2.1000436)
Opened by the GWR 2 December 1889, closed by BR on 5 March 1956, reopened as *Culkerton Halt* 2 February 1959, renamed as *Culkerton* May 1959 and closed 6 April 1964.

CURRIEHILL (CUH)

Curriehill Road, Currie, Edinburgh EH14 5PS
NT1763668267 (55.900449, -3.3188177)
Opened by the CR 15 February 1848 as *Currie*, renamed as *Currie Hill* 1 May 1874, closed by BR 2 April 1951 and reopened 5 October 1987 as *Curriehill*.
ASR 2CD**HPS** **66,722**

CUSTOM HOUSE

Location: TQ4070180942 (51.509898, 0.026095212)
Opened by the Eastern Counties Railway 26 November 1855, closed by Railtrack 29 May 1994, reopened 29 October 1995 and closed 10 December 2006.

CWMBACH (CMH)

Looking north on 10 May 2015.

Cwmbach Road, Cwmbach, Rhondda Cynon Taff CF44 0AG
SO0232301257 (51.701529, -3.4148195)
Opened by the GWR 12 July 1914 as *Cwmbach Halt*, closed by BR 15 June 1964 and rebuilt and reopened as *Cwmbach* 3 October 1988.
ATW 1CD**HS** **22,798**

CWMBRAN (CWM)

Looking south along Platform 2 on 24 May 2015.

Somerset Industrial Estate, Cwmbran, Torfaen NP44 1QX
ST2981095904 (51.657516, -3.0160823)
Opened 12 May 1986.
ATW 2CD**HPS**T**TW** **386,224**

DAIMLER HALT

Location: SP3315080250 (52.419244, -1.5139921)
Opened by the L&NWR 19 March 1917 for factory employees, opened by BR for regular passenger traffic 11 June 1956 and closed 18 January 1965.

DALGETY BAY (DAG)

Clockluine Road, Dalgety Bay, Dunfermline, Fife KY11 9HZ
NT1493984116 (56.042334, -3.3669394)
Opened 28 March 1998.
ASR 2CD**HPS**T **315,212**

DALMARNOCK (DAK)

Swanston Street, Dalmarnock, Glasgow G40 4HG
NS6124563207 (55.842064, -4.2174666)
Opened by the Glasgow Central Railway 1 November 1895, closed by BR 5 October 1964 and reopened 5 November 1979.
ASR 2C**DHS**T **367,722**

DALSTON JUNCTION (DLJ) **X**

Dalston Lane, London E8 3DE
TQ3357184776 (51.546078, -0.075124651)
Opened by the North London Railway 1 November 1865, closed by BR 30 June 1986 and reopened 27 April 2010.
LO 4CD**H**R**STT** **5,296,838**

DALSTON KINGSLAND (DLK) X

Looking west on 4 June 2016.

Kingsland High Road, Dalston, London E8 2JS
TQ3352885008 (51.548177, -0.075655013)
Opened by the North London Railway 9 November 1850 as *Kingsland*, closed 1 November 1865 and reopened by BR 16 May 1983 as *Dalston Kingsland*.
LO 2C**HS**TT **6,184,348**

DALVEY FARM HALT

Location: NJ1107032157 (57.371151, -3.4803430)
One of four halts opened on the Speyside route between Elgin and Aviemore on 15 June 1959, on the introduction of railbuses, and closed 18 October 1965 when services on the line were withdrawn.

DANESCOURT (DCT)

Looking north along Platform 1 on 24 May 2015.

Llantrisant Road, Cardiff CF5 2RX
ST1445078671 (51.500477, -3.2338791)
Opened 4 October 1987.
ATW 2CD**PS**T **107,740**

DEE STREET HALT

Location: NO69699 95547 (57.049992, -2.5010821)
Opened 6 February 1961 and closed 28 February 1966.

DEIGHTON (DHN)

Looking north along Platform 2 on 18 June 2016. The first station at Deighton was located on the north side of the road bridge and was opened by the L&NWR 30 August 1871 and closed by the LM&SR 28 July 1930.

Whitacre Street, Deighton, Huddersfield,
West Yorkshire HD2 1LX
SE1646019123 (53.668325, -1.7523529)
Opened 26 April 1982.
NR 2C**DS 95,070**

DENT (DNT)

Viewed on 31 May 2015, this station is the highest one on the National Rail network in England at 1,150ft above sea level.

Station Approach, Coal Road, Cowgill, Cumbria LA10 5RF
SD7641787509 (54.282671, -2.3637289)
Opened by the MR 6 August 1877, closed by BR 4 May 1970 and reopened 14 July 1986.
NR 2D**HPS 7,248**

DIGBY & SOWTON (DIG)

Class 153 Unit No.153325 about to depart from the station on 25 May 2017. This station is sited about 350 yards south of *Clyst St Mary and Digby Halt* which was opened by the L&SWR 1 June 1908 and closed by BR 27 September 1948.

Digby Drive, Digby, Exeter, Devon EX2 7QF
SX9606191524 (50.714025, -3.4735747)
Opened 29 May 1995.
GWR 1**DHPST 588,944**

DODWORTH (DOD)

Class 144 Unit No.144018 approaching the station on 7 May 2016.

Station Road, Dodworth, Barnsley, South Yorkshire S75 3JX
SE3110005385 (53.544190, -1.5321448)
Opened by the Manchester, Sheffield and Lincolnshire Railway 1 July 1854, closed by BR 29 June 1959 and reopened 15 May 1989.
NR 1**CPS 46,244**

DOLGARROG (DLG)

Off Llanwrst Road, Dolgarrog, Conwy LL26 0YR
SH7827866972 (53.185873, -3.8230745)

Viewed from the level crossing on 16 July 2015.

Opened by the L&NWR 18 December 1916, closed by BR 26 October 1964 and reopened 14 June 1965.
ATW 1**CHPS 1,002**

DRAYTON PARK (DYP)

Looking south on 22 August 2017. This station became part of the LPTE in 1933 and was transferred to BR 5 October 1975.

Drayton Park, Highbury, London N5 1NT
TQ3142185521 (51.553273, -0.10583049)
Opened by the Great Northern and City Railway 14 February 1904, closed by the LPTE 5 October 1975 and reopened by BR 16 August 1976.
GN 2**CHSTT 791,700**

DRONFIELD (DRO)

Looking south along Platform 2 on 28 January 2015.

Chesterfield Road, Dronfield, Derbyshire S18 2XG
SK3544578417 (53.301524, -1.4696065)
Opened by the MR 1 February 1870, closed by BR 2 January 1967 and reopened 5 January 1981.
NR 2CD**HPS** 209,430

DRUMFROCHAR (DFR)

Lemmon Street, Drumfrochar, Greenock, Inverclyde PA15 4HT
NS2695275493 (55.941236, -4.7723284)
Opened 24 May 1998.
ASR 1CD**HS** 80,654

DRUMGELLOCH

Location: NS7759565367 (55.865886, -3.9575237) (Approx)
Opened 15 May 1989 and closed 9 May 2010.

DRUMGELLOCH (DRU)

Meadowside Place, Airdrie, North Lanarkshire ML6 7AW
NS7776065378 (55.866029, -3.9548856)
Opened 6 March 2011. This station occupies the site of *Clarkston* station which was opened by the Bathgate and Coatbridge Railway 11 August 1862, renamed as *Clarkston (Lanarks)* by BR 8 June 1953 and closed 9 January 1956.
ASR 2CD**HPS**T 411,086

DRUMRY (DMY)

Onslow Drive, Drumry, Clydebank, West Dunbartonshire G81 2PJ
NS5096470512 (55.904571, -4.3855257)
Opened 6 April 1953.
ASR 2CD**HS**T 251,204

DUMBRECK (DUM)

Nithsdale Road, Dumbreck, Glasgow G41 5AH
NS5600963672 (55.844699, -4.3012601)
Opened by the G&SWR 1 July 1885 as *Bellahouston*, closed 1 January 1917, reopened in August 1920, closed by BR 20 September 1954, and reopened 30 July 1990 as *Dumbreck*.
ASR 2CD**HS**T 169,702

DUNCRAIG (DCG)

Duncraig, Highland IV52 8TZ
NG8120333228 (57.336899, -5.6371906)
Opened 2 November 1897 as a private station by the HR and named as *Duncraig Platform*, it was opened to the public by BR 23 May 1949, renamed as *Duncraig* 10 September 1962, closed 7 December 1964 and reopened 5 January 1976. The station, which is Category B listed, is signposted off a minor road and the track to the station is a continuation of the drive to Duncraig Castle.
ASR 1**HS** 348

DUNFERMLINE QUEEN MARGARET (DFL)

Hill of St Margaret, Off Whitefield Road,
Dunfermline KY12 0GB
NT1165788425 (56.080445, -3.4210262)
Opened 26 January 2000.
ASR 2CD**HPS**T 236,652

DUNLOP (DNL)

Station Road, Dunlop, Kilmarnock, East Ayrshire KA3 4AS
NS4099849408 (55.711953, -4.5324250)
Opened by the Glasgow, Barrhead and Kilmarnock Joint Railway 27 March 1871, closed by BR 7 November 1966 and reopened 5 June 1967 as a single-line unstaffed halt. Following track doubling in 2008, a second platform was added along with improved disabled access and a car park.
ASR 2CD**HPS**T 91,990

DUNROBIN CASTLE (DNO)

A9, Dunrobin, Brora, Highland KW10 6SF
NC8496401285 (57.985872, -3.9471844)
Opened by the Duke of Sutherland's Railway 1 November 1870 as *Dunrobin*, closed to the public 19 June 1871, reopened on an unrecorded date, closed by BR 29 January 1965 and reopened 30 June 1985. It was renamed as *Dunrobin Castle* 17 May 1993 and remains in the ownership of Sutherland Estates.
ASR 1D**HS** 882

DUNSTON (DOT)

Looking east on 25 September 2015.

Ellison Road, Dunston, Newcastle upon Tyne NE11 9SS
NZ2304461771 (54.950060, -1.6417453)
Opened by the NER 1 January 1909 as *Dunston-on-Tyne*, closed
1 May 1918, reopened 1 October 1919, closed by the L&NER
4 May 1926 and reopened by BR 1 October 1984 as *Dunston*.
NR 2CD**HS** 10,618

DYCE (DYC)
Station Road, Dyce, Aberdeenshire AB21 7BA
NJ8845612790 (57.205734, -2.1927246)
Opened by the Great North of Scotland Railway 18 June 1861,
closed by BR 6 May 1968 and reopened 15 September 1984. On
the opening of the Buchan line, this station replaced the original
one which was located 350 yards to the north and had opened
20 September 1854.
ASR 2CD**HPS**T 517,586

EASTBROOK (EBK)

Viewed on 24 May 2015.

Cardiff Road, Dinas Powys, Vale of Glamorgan CF64 4LD
ST1626171682 (51.437919, -3.2061276)
Opened 24 November 1986.
ATW 2CD**HPS**T 174,262

EASTER ROAD PARK HALT
Location: On Leith Central Branch
Opened 8 April 1950, closed 4 January 1964 and only used for
detraining football traffic.

EAST GARFORTH (EGF)

Class 153 Unit No.153343 departing from the station on 17 May 2016.

Woodlands Drive, Garforth, Leeds LS25 2JW
SE4154133045 (53.792067, -1.3709065)
Opened 1 May 1987.
NR 2CD**ST** 252,948

EASTHAM RAKE (ERA)

Viewed on 17 May 2015.

Eastham Rake, Birkenhead, Wirral CH62 9AL
SJ3471479401 (53.307506, -2.9812351)
Opened 3 April 1995.
M 2C**HPRST** 303,060

EAST MIDLANDS PARKWAY (EMD)

Looking south on 2 April 2016.

Off A453, Near Ratcliffe-on-Soar, Nottingham NG11 0EE
SK4972929670 (52.862225, -1.2628001)
Opened 26 January 2009.
EMT 4AC**DHPRRSTTW** 347,252

EBBSFLEET INTERNATIONAL (EBD)

Looking east along Platform 5 on 13 September 2017.

International Way, Ebbsfleet Valley, Dartford, Kent DA10 1EB
TQ6140674192 (51.443720, 0.32113150)
Opened 19 November 2007.
SE 6**ABCDH**PRST**TW** 1,846,538

EBBW VALE PARKWAY (EBV)

Looking south on 24 May 2015.

Off Glan Ebbw Terrace, Victoria, Ebbw Vale, Blaenau Gwent
NP23 8AP
SO1754007090 (51.756405, -3.1960747)
Opened 6 February 2008.
ATW 1**CDH**PST 57,108

EBBW VALE TOWN (EBB)

Steelworks Road, Ebbw Vale, Blaenau Gwent NP23 6DN
SO1685009950 (51.782011, -3.206749)

Class 150 Unit No.150260 approaching the station on 24 May 2015.

Opened 17 May 2015.
ATW 1**CDH**ST 232,206

EDINBURGH GATEWAY (EGY) **X**

1 Myreton Drive, Gogar, Edinburgh EH12 9GF
NT1768572756 (55.940777, -3.3194000)
Built as part of the Edinburgh to Glasgow Improvement
Programme and opened on 11 December 2016. The station
was heavily vandalized on the night of 11 June 2016 and is an
interchange with Edinburgh Trams.
ASR 2**CDH**STW 58,386

EDINBURGH PARK (EDP) **X**

Cultins Road, Edinburgh EH11 4DF
NT1838271273 (55.927576, -3.3077940)
Opened 4 December 2003. This station is an interchange with
Edinburgh Trams.
ASR 2**CDH**ST 869,978

ELTHAM (ELW) **X**

Looking north along Platform 2 on 14 May 2016. This station replaced
two others which both closed on the day that Eltham opened; *Eltham
Well Hall* which was sited 220 yards to the west and was opened by
the Blackheath Railway as *Well Hall* 1 May 1895, renamed as *Well Hall
for North Eltham* by the SE&CR 1 October 1916 and as *Eltham Well Hall*
by the SR 26 September 1927. *Eltham Park*, sited 500 yards to the east,
was opened by the SE&CR 1 July 1908 as *Shooter's Hill and Eltham Park*
and renamed as *Eltham Park* by the SR 26 September 1927.

Well Hall Road, London SE9 1SA
TQ4268174958 (51.455631, 0.052203834)
Opened 17 March 1985.
SE 2**AB**CD**H**PR**STTW** **2,387,308**

ENERGLYN & CHURCHILL PARK (ECP)

Looking north along Platform 2 on 2 August 2015. The disposition of the station is such that the northbound platform (No.2) is in Energlyn and No.1 is in Churchill Park!

Llwyn-on Street, Caerphilly CF83 2QR
ST1494687965 (51.584102, -3.2289787)
Opened 8 December 2013. The station was formally opened 16 December 2013 by Edwina Hart, Welsh Government Transport Minister.
ATW 2CD**HS**T **86,422**

EPSOM DOWNS (EPD)

Class 455 Unit No.455827 at the buffer stops on 23 July 2016. This station replaced the original one, opened by the LB&SCR 22 May 1865 and closed by BR 11 February 1989 when the branch was truncated by 300 yards.

Bunbury Way, Longdown Lane, Epsom, Surrey KT17 4JP
TQ2282859800 (51.324050, -0.23863211)
Opened 13 February 1989.
So 1CD**HS**T **90,840**

ESKBANK (EKB)

Unit 4, Hardengreen Industrial Estate, Dalkeith EH22 3NX
NT3234965804 (55.880613, -3.0829471)
Opened 6 September 2015. The original station, sited to the south, was opened by the NBR 21 June 1847 as *Gallowshall*, renamed as *Eskbank* in October 1850, as *Eskbank and Dalkeith* by BR in January 1954 and closed 6 January 1969.
ASR 1CD**HP**S**T** **274,770**

ESSEX ROAD (EXR)

181 Essex Road, Islington, London N1 2SU
TQ3211484132 (51.540633, -0.096365500) (Subterranean)
Opened by the Great Northern and City Railway 14 February 1904, renamed as *Canonbury and Essex Road* 20 July 1922, reverted back to *Essex Road* by the LPTE 11 July 1948, closed by the LPTE 5 October 1975 and reopened by BR 16 August 1976.
GN 2C**HS**T **810,518**

EUXTON BALSHAW LANE (EBA)

Looking north on 26 April 2016.

Balshaw Lane, Euxton, Lancashire PR7 6HY
SD5570718387 (53.660083, -2.6717296)
Opened by the L&NWR 2 September 1905 as *Balshaw Lane and Euxton*, closed by BR 6 October 1969 and reopened 15 December 1997 as *Euxton Balshaw Lane*.
NR 2D**HP**S **77,156**

EXHIBITION CENTRE (GLASGOW) (EXG) **X**

Minerva Street, Glasgow G3 8JR
NS5723465475 (55.861250, -4.2826620)
Opened by the CR 10 August 1896 as *Stobcross*, closed by BR 3 August 1959, reopened 5 November 1979 as *Finnieston* and renamed as *Exhibition Centre* in 1986.
ASR 2CD**HST**W **1,891,500**

EXMOUTH (EXM)

Class 153 Unit No.153382 at the buffer stops on 25 May 2017. The original station was opened by the Exeter and Exmouth Railway 1 May 1861 and closed by BR 2 May 1976 when the branch line was slightly shortened.

Marine Way, Exmouth, Devon EX8 1BZ
SY0000281216 (50.622049, -3.4149899)
Opened 2 May 1976.
GWR 1BCDHPSTT **960,370**

EYEMOUTH

Location: NT94396388 (55.868060, -2.0912152)
Opened by the Eyemouth Railway on 13 April 1891, closed due to flood damage by BR 13 August 1948, reopened 29 June 1949 and closed 5 February 1962.

FAIRWATER (FRW)

Viewed on 24 May 2015.

Pwllmelin Road, Cardiff CF5 2NH
ST1443677955 (51.494038, -3.2339032)
Opened 4 October 1987.
ATW 2CDST **77,216**

FALLS OF CRUACHAN (FOC)

A85, Falls of Cruachan, Dalmally, Argyll & Bute PA33 1AN
NN0782226870 (56.394887, -5.1152790)
Opened by the Callander and Oban Railway 1 October 1893, closed by BR 1 November 1965, reopened 20 June 1988 and, as it is not installed with lighting, is only open during the summer months.
ASR 1HS **734**

FALMOUTH DOCKS (FAL)

Class 150 Unit No.150124 at the buffer stops on 24 May 2017. This station closed when the branch line was truncated by 924 yards and reopened when the line was reinstated.

Station Approach, Pendennis Rise, Falmouth,
Cornwall TR11 4LT
SW8178632324 (50.150730, -5.0559023)
Opened by the Cornwall Railway 24 August 1863 as *Falmouth*, closed by BR 7 December 1970, reopened 5 May 1975 and renamed as *Falmouth Docks* in October 1988.
GWR 1DHPS **99,610**

FALMOUTH TOWN (FMT)

Looking north on 24 May 2017. This station was opened when the branch line was truncated by 924 yards and the original terminus station (*Falmouth*, later *Falmouth Docks* [qv]) closed 7 December 1970. The line was reinstated 5 May 1975.

Avenue Road, Falmouth, Cornwall TR11 4AZ
SW8114232085 (50.148344, -5.0647643)
Opened 7 December 1970 as *Falmouth*, renamed as *The Dell*
5 May 1975 and as *Falmouth Town* in October 1988.
GWR 1H**PS 208,218**

FEATHERSTONE (FEA)

Looking east along Platform 2 on 7 May 2016 with Platform 1 in view on the other side of the level crossing. Although officially closed to passengers on 2 January 1967, the station remained open for irregular traffic until c May 1975.

Station Lane, Featherstone, Pontefract, West Yorkshire WF7 6EG
SE4247820481 (53.679071, -1.3583981)
Opened by the Wakefield, Pontefract and Goole Railway 1 April 1848, closed by BR 2 January 1967 and reopened 11 May 1992.
NR 2CD**HS 65,260**

FENITON (FNT)

Ottery Road, Feniton, Honiton, Devon EX14 3BT
SY0949899346 (50.786597, -3.2852380)

Looking west on 25 May 2017 with the abandoned eastbound platform in view on the right.

Opened by the L&SWR 19 July 1860, renamed as *Ottery and Sidmouth Road* 1 July 1861, as *Feniton for Ottery St Mary* in February 1868, as *Ottery Road* in April 1868, as *Sidmouth Junction* 6 July 1874, closed by BR 6 March 1967 and reopened 3 May 1971 as *Feniton*.
SWR 1CD**HPSTT 69,078**

FERNHILL (FER)

Viewed on 10 May 2015.

Aberdare Road, Fernhill, Rhondda Cynon Taff CF45 3DG
ST0360599568 (51.686567, -3.3958147)
Opened 3 October 1988.
ATW 1CD**PS 24,520**

FILTON ABBEY WOOD (FIT)

Looking south along Platform 2 on 7 June 2015. The first station, located just north of this one, was opened by the Bristol and South Wales Union Railway 8 September 1863 as *Filton* and closed 4 October 1886. The second, built 11 chains north of the first, was opened by the GWR 4 October 1886 as *Filton*, renamed as *Filton Junction* 1 May 1910, reverted back to *Filton* by BR 6 May 1968 and used Saturdays only until closure 31 May 1997.

Emma-Chris Way, Filton, Bristol BS34 7JW
ST6095478411 (51.503273, -2.5639316)
Opened 11 March 1996.
GWR 3CD**HPSTT 1,064,634**

FISHGUARD & GOODWICK (FGW)

Station Hill, Goodwick, Pembrokeshire SA64 0DG
SM9453338204 (52.004150, -4.9948646)

Looking west on 14 June 2017. After closure to regular traffic on 6 April 1964 it was used for workmen's trains until 3 August 1964.

Opened by the GWR 1 July 1899 as *Goodwick*, renamed as *Fishguard and Goodwick* 1 May 1904, closed to regular passenger traffic by BR 6 April 1964 and totally 3 August 1964. It was reopened as a seasonal terminus for Motorail trains 18 June 1965, closed again 16 September 1972 and rebuilt and reopened 14 May 2012.
ATW 1C**DP**S**T** 19,600

FITZWILLIAM (FZW)

Looking along Platform 1 on 7 May 2016. *Fitzwilliam Halt*, opened by the L&NER 1 June 1937, renamed as *Fitzwilliam* 16 June 1947 and closed by BR 6 November 1967, was sited to the north of this station.

Railway Terrace, Fitzwilliam, Pontefract,
West Yorkshire WF9 5DA
SE4146615286 (53.632460, -1.3744149)
Opened 1 March 1982.
NR 2C**DHPS**T 302,122

FIVE WAYS (FWY) X

Class 323 Unit No.323218 about to depart for Birmingham New Street from Platform 1 on 18 July 2015.

Islington Row, Edgbaston, Birmingham B15 1QA
SP0599685887 (52.470890, -1.9131580)
Opened by the MR 1 July 1885, closed as a wartime measure by the LM&SR from 2 October 1944 and officially closed by BR in October 1950, it was rebuilt and reopened 8 May 1978.
WMT 2C**DHS**T**TW** 1,660,958

FLOWERY FIELD (FLF)

Viewed on 28 June 2015.

Bennett Street, Hyde, Greater Manchester SK14 4TF
SJ9475396095 (53.461577, -2.0804983)
Opened 13 May 1985.
NR 2C**S** 222,152

FORD GREEN

Location: SJ88700 50700 (53.053435, -2.1700336)
Opened by the Potteries Biddulph & Congleton Railway 1 June 1864, renamed as *Ford Green and Smallthorne* c1887, closed to passengers by the LM&SR 11 July 1927, reopened for excursion traffic by BR as *Ford Green* prior to July 1960 and closed after August 1962.

FORRES (FOR)

Station Road, Off A96, Forres, Highland IV36 3AD
NJ03012 59040 (57.610889, -3.6249572)
Opened on 17 October 2017 when the track was reconstructed on a new alignment bypassing the second station which had been opened by the Inverness & Aberdeen Junction Railway 3 August 1863 and closed 5 October 2017.
ASR 2**CDHPS**S**TTW** N/A

FORT MATILDA (FTM)

Newark Street, Fort Matilda, Greenock, Inverclyde PA16 7TS
NS2560977521 (55.958955, -4.7951165)
Opened by the CR 1 June 1889, it was closed temporarily by BR for tunnel repairs between 5 February and 20 April 1973 prior to permanent closure 3 October 1993 and reopened 27 March 1995.
ASR 2**CDHPS** 140,472

FORT WILLIAM (FTW)

Tom-na-Faire, Station Square, Fort William,
Highland PH33 6AN
NN1060874218 (56.820764, -5.1049036)
Opened 9 June 1975. The original station, sited 880 yards to the south-west, was opened by the West Highland Railway 7 August 1894.
ASR 2**BCDHPRSTW** 138,514

FOWEY

Location: SX12664 52304 (50.340791, -4.6340820)
Opened by the Cornish Mineral Railway 20 June 1876, closed by the GWR 1 January 1880, reopened 16 September 1865, closed 1 January 1940, reopened 9 February 1942, closed by BR 4 January 1965, reopened 29 May 1994 and closed 5 September 1994.

FRIZINGHALL (FZH)

Looking north along Platform 2 on 18 June 2016. As originally built the two platforms were sited on the north side of Frizinghall Road but, since reopening, the southbound platform (No.2) is now on the south side of the road.

Frizinghall, Bradford, West Yorkshire BD9 4JB
SE1530436041 (53.820425, -1.7690107)
Opened by the MR 1 February 1875, closed by BR 22 March 1965 and reopened 7 September 1987.
NR 2**CDHPS**T 440,964

GALASHIELS (GAL)

Ladhope Vale, Galashiels, Scottish Borders TD1 1BP
NT4934136338 (55.617982, -2.8058964)
Opened 6 September 2015. The original Galashiels Station, sited to the south, was opened by the NBR 20 February 1849 and closed by BR 6 January 1969.
ASR 1**CDHS**T 346,264

GARSCADDEN (GRS)

Kinellar Drive, Garscadden, Glasgow G14 0EY
NS5224368560 (55.887443, -4.3640211)
Opened 7 November 1960.
ASR 2**CHST** 209,064

GARSDALE (GSD)

Viewed on 31 May 2015.

Off A684, Garsdale Head, Near Sedbergh, Cumbria LA10 5PP
SD7887591818 (54.321504, -2.3262772)
Opened by the MR 1 August 1876 as *Hawes Junction*, renamed as *Hawes Junction and Garsdale* 20 January 1900, as *Garsdale* by the LM&SR 1 September 1932, closed by BR 4 May 1970 and reopened 14 July 1986.
NR 2**DHSW** 12,520

GARSTON (HERTFORDSHIRE) (GSN)

Fourth Avenue, Garston, Watford, Hertfordshire WD25 9QG
TQ1196499893 (51.686643, -0.38175210)
Opened 7 February 1966.
WMT 1**CDHS** 72,670

Looking north on 23 July 2017.

GARTCOSH (GRH)

Craignethan Drive, Gartcosh, North Lanarkshire G69 8AA
NS7005867781 (55.885590, -4.0790257)
Opened by the Garnkirk and Glasgow Railway 1 June 1831, closed by BR 5 November 1962 and rebuilt and reopened 9 May 2005.
ASR 2CD**HPS**T 133,838

GARTH (MID-GLAMORGAN) (GMG)

Viewed on 2 August 2015. A previous station, *Troedyrhiew Garth*, which was opened by the Llynvi Valley Railway 25 February 1864 and closed by BR 15 July 1970, was sited to the south of this one.

Mill Street, Garth, Maesteg, Bridgend CF34 9HS
SS8629989940 (51.596790, -3.6429186)
Opened 28 September 1992.
ATW 1CD**PS** 12,036

GILBEY'S COTTAGES HALT

Location: NJ1931041574 (57.457253, -3.3464772
One of four halts opened on the Speyside route between Elgin and Aviemore on 15 June 1959, on the introduction of railbuses, and closed 18 October 1965 when services on the line were withdrawn.

GILSHOCHILL (GSC)

Cadder Road, Gilshochill, Glasgow G23 5LF
NS5737469486 (55.897303, -4.2825410)
Opened 3 December 1993 as *Lambhill* and renamed as *Gilshochill* 24 May 1998.
ASR 2C**HS** 65,076

GLAN CONWY (GCW)

Looking south on 16 July 2015.

Conway Road, Glan Conwy, Conwy LL28 5ED
SH8021276137 (53.268656, -3.7975976)
Opened by the Conway and Llanrwst Railway 17 June 1863 as *Llansaintffraid*, renamed as *Glan Conway* by the L&NWR 1 January 1865, closed by BR 26 October 1964, reopened 4 May 1970 and renamed as *Glan Conwy* 12 May 1980.
ATW 1CD**HPS** 3,566

GLASGOW CENTRAL (LOW LEVEL) (GLC) X

Gordon Street, Glasgow G1 3SL
NS5877365238 (55.859580, -4.2579612) (Subterranean)
Opened by the Glasgow Central Railway 10 August 1896, closed by BR 5 October 1964 and reopened 5 November 1979.
ASR 2**ABC**D**HPRS**TT**W** N/A

GLASSHOUGHTON (GLH)

Looking north along Platform 2 on 7 May 2016.

Colorado Way, Glasshoughton, Castleford,
West Yorkshire WF10 4TA
SE4353423833 (53.709113, -1.3419387)
Opened 21 February 2005.
NR 2CD**HPS** 186,498

GLEN DOUGLAS HALT
Location: NS2742999419 (56.156127, -4.7801172)
Opened by West Highland Railway 7 August 1894 as *Glen Douglas Platform*, closed to regular passenger traffic by the L&NER by September 1926, renamed as *Glen Douglas* by May 1942, reopened to regular passenger traffic as *Glen Douglas Halt* by BR 12 June 1961 and closed 15 June 1964.

GLENROTHES WITH THORNTON (GLT)
Main Street, Thornton, Fife KY1 4AE
NT2912897219 (56.162353, -3.1427175)
Opened 11 May 1992.
ASR 2CD**HPSX** 76,916

GODLEY (GDL)

Viewed on 28 June 2015, this is built on the site of *Godley Toll Bar* station which was opened by the Sheffield, Ashton-under-Lyne and Manchester Railway 17 November 1841 and closed 11 December 1842.

Mottram Road, Hyde, Tameside,
Greater Manchester SK14 3GA
SJ9640095058 (53.452268, -2.0556812)
Opened 7 July 1986.
NR 2**S** 82,954

GOLDTHORPE (GOE)

Viewed on 16 April 2016.

Barnsley Road, Goldthorpe, Rotherham,
South Yorkshire S63 9BS
SE4564004369 (53.533998, -1.3128796)
Opened 16 May 1988.
NR 2D**HPS** 61,788

GOLF STREET (GOF)
Golf Street, Carnoustie, Angus DD7 7JH
NO5576734221 (56.497978, -2.7200885)
Opened 7 November 1960 as *Golf Street Halt* and renamed as *Golf Street* 16 May 1983.
ASR 2D**S** 104

GOREBRIDGE (GBH)
Station Road, Gorebridge EH23 4JX
NT3456561266 (55.840154, -3.0464248)
Opened by the NBR 14 July 1847, closed by BR 6 January 1969 and rebuilt and reopened 6 September 2015.
ASR 1CD**HPST** 98,218

GRAIN
Location: TQ8679474952 (51.442750, 0.68643898) (Approx)
Opened 4 September 1951 and closed 4 December 1961.

GREENFAULDS (GRL)
Greenfaulds Road, Greenfaulds, Cumbernauld G67 2XJ
NS7555673117 (55.934954, -3.9936429)
Opened 15 May 1989.
ASR 2D**HPSTW** 114,784

GRETNA GREEN (GEA)
Glasgow Road, Gretna Green, Dumfries & Galloway DG16 5DU
NY3183267867 (55.000687, -3.0671925)
Opened 20 September 1993. This station replaced one sited just to the east which was opened by the Glasgow, Dumfries and Carlisle Railway 23 August 1848 as *Gretna*, renamed as *Gretna Green* by the G&SWR in April 1852 and closed by BR 6 December 1965.
ASR 2CD**HPS** 39,042

GUNNISLAKE (GSL)

Looking north to the buffer stops on 23 May 2017. This station replaced the original one, which was sited on the opposite side of the road bridge and opened by the Plymouth, Devonport and South Western Junction Railway 2 March 1908 and closed by BR 31 January 1994.

Sand Hill, Gunnislake, Cornwall PL18 9DT
SX4275470858 (50.516336, -4.2193656)
Opened 9 June 1994.
GWR 1D**HPS 54,510**

GYPSY LANE (GYP)

Looking south on 26 September 2015.

Gypsy Lane, Nunthorpe, Middlesbrough, Redcar and Cleveland
TS7 0DY
NZ5319115605 (54.532933, -1.1795363)
Opened 3 May 1976.
NR 1CD**HS 32,996**

HACKNEY CENTRAL (HKC) X

Viewed on 4 June 2016.

Amhurst Road, Hackney, Greater London E8 1NA
TQ3481484920 (51.547076, -0.057160556)
Opened by the North London Railway 1 December 1870 as
Hackney, closed by the LM&SR 23 April 1945 and reopened by
BR 12 May 1980 as *Hackney Central.*
LO 2CD**HPSTT 4,829,020**

HACKNEY WICK (HKW)

Looking along Platform 2 on 4 June 2016.

Wallis Road, Greater London E9 5LH
TQ3709684577 (51.543446, -0.024405420)
Opened 12 May 1980.
LO 2CD**HSTT 2,140,198**

HADDENHAM & THAME PARKWAY (HDM)

Looking north on 2 July 2017.

Thame Road, Haddenham, Buckinghamshire HP17 8NX
SP7306508600 (51.771312, -0.94250143)
Opened 5 October 1987.
ChR 2CD**HPRSTTW 849,150**

HADNOCK HALT
Location: SO5288914847 (51.830240, -2.6850490)
Opened 7 May 1951 and closed 5 January 1959.

HAG FOLD (HGF)

Looking along Platform 2 on 9 April 2017.

Spa Road, Atherton, Greater Manchester M46 9WX
SD6734604227 (53.533673, -2.4941258)
Opened 11 May 1987.
NR 2CD**HST** 50,212

HAGGERSTON (HGG) X

Class 378 Unit No.378145 on Platform 2 on 9 July 2016. The first Haggerston station, sited immediately to the south, was opened by the North London Railway 2 September 1867 and closed by the LM&SR 6 May 1940.

Lee Street, London E8 4DY
TQ3356283976 (51.538892, -0.075555146)
Opened 27 April 2010.
LO 2C**DH**R**STT** 3,223,048

HALEWOOD (HED)

Hollies Road, Halewood, Merseyside L26 0UG
SJ4489185623 (53.364593, -2.8296152)
Opened 16 May 1988.
NR 2CD**HST** 118,494

Viewed on 10 August 2016.

HALL-I'-TH'-WOOD (HID)

Crompton Way, Hall-i'-th'-Wood, Bolton, Lancashire BL2 3AD
SD7275711295 (53.597513, -2.4131057)
Opened 29 September 1986.
NR 2**HPS** 157,280

HARDLEY HALT

Location: SU4430205861 (50.850579, -1.3720519) (Approx)
Opened 3 March 1958 and closed 5 April 1965.

HATTERSLEY (HTY)

Looking west on 28 June 2015.

Hattersley Road, Hattersley, Hyde,
Greater Manchester SK14 3LQ
SJ9745394257 (53.445075, -2.0398200)
Opened 8 May 1978.
NR 2**PST** 78,956

HAWKHEAD (HKH)

Hawkhead Road, Hawkhead, Paisley, Renfrewshire PA1 1RE
NS4984963595 (55.842133, -4.3995041)

Opened by the G&SWR 1 May 1894, closed 1 January 1917, reopened 10 February 1919, closed by BR 14 February 1966 and rebuilt and reopened 12 April 1991.
ASR 1CD**HPS**T **224,040**

HEDGE END (HDE)

Viewed on 2 October 2015.

Stroudley Way, Grange Park, Hedge End, Southampton SO30 2RZ
SU4966915014 (50.932445, -1.2945709)
Opened 6 May 1990.
SWR 2C**HPST** **511,852**

HEDNESFORD (HNF)

Looking north on 22 July 2015. At the time of reopening Hednesford station was a temporary terminus and only Platform 1, in view in the foreground, was rebuilt and operational but following the extension of the line through to Rugeley in 1997 Platform 2 was brought into use.

Market Street, Hednesford, Cannock, Staffordshire WS12 4FA
SJ9996312477 (52.709955, -2.0019847)
Opened by the Cannock Mineral Railway in January 1860 and worked from the outset by the L&NWR, it was closed by BR 18 January 1965 and reopened 10 April 1989.
WMT 2CD**HPS**T **179,000**

HEDON SPEEDWAY HALT

Location: TA1694929411 (53.747962, -0.22801191)
Opened by the NER 24 August 1888 as *Hedon Racecourse*, closed c1909, reopened by BR 14 August 1948 as *Hedon Speedway Halt* and closed 23 October 1948.

HELSBY AND ALVANLEY

Location: SJ4862274742 (53.267167, -2.7717760)
Opened by the West Cheshire Railway 22 June 1870, closed 1 May 1875, reopened 3 May 1934, closed 22 May 1944, reopened by BR 9 September 1963 and closed 6 January 1964.

HEWORTH (HEW)

Looking west on 25 September 2015. This is also an interchange station with Tyne Metro.

Heworth Interchange, Sunderland Road, Gateshead NE10 0NE
NZ2854161982 (54.951677, -1.5558985)
Opened 5 November 1979.
NR 2D**HS** **20,784**

HEYSHAM PORT (HHB)

Looking west to the buffer stops on 20 September 2015. The original station was opened on an adjacent site by the MR 11 July 1904 as *Heysham Harbour* and closed by BR 4 May 1970. It was subsequently demolished to accommodate alterations to the quayside to facilitate changes to the type of ferries used by the operator Sealink.

Station Road, Heysham, Lancashire LA3 2XE
SD4033660113 (54.033530, -2.9124257)
Opened 4 May 1970 as *Heysham Harbour*, closed 6 October 1975, reopened 11 May 1987 as *Heysham Sea Terminal*, renamed as *Heysham Port* by 11 May 1992, closed 8 February 1994 and reopened 16 December 1994.
NR 1D**PS** 10,158

HIGHBURY & ISLINGTON (LOW LEVEL) (HHY) X
Holloway Road, London N5 1RA
TQ3152484713 (51.545988, -0.10465711) (Subterranean)
Opened by the Great Northern and City Railway 28 June 1904, closed by the LPTE 5 October 1975 and reopened by BR 16 August 1976.
LU 2C**HST** N/A

HIGH STREET (GLASGOW) (HST)
High Street, Glasgow G1 1PZ
NS5988765193 (55.859499, -4.2401621)
Opened by the Glasgow City & District Railway 1 April 1871 as *College*, renamed as *High Street* by the NBR 1 January 1914, closed 1977 by BR and reopened 5 October 1981.
ASR 2C**HRST** 857,586

HOMERTON (HMN) X

Looking east along Platform 2 on 4 June 2016.

Barnabas Road, Homerton, Greater London E9 5SB
TQ3579284948 (51.547096, -0.043041408)
Opened by the North London Railway 1 October 1868, closed by the LM&SR 23 April 1945 and reopened by BR 13 May 1985.
LO 2CD**HSTT** 4,815,576

HONEYBOURNE (HVB)
Station Road, Honeybourne, Worcestershire WR11 7GL
SP1147344831 (52.101701, -1.8339148)
Opened by the Oxford, Worcester and Wolverhampton Railway 4 June 1853, closed by BR 5 May 1969 and reopened 25 May 1981.
GWR 2CD**HPS** 59,496

Looking west along Platform 1 on 5 October 2015. By the time of reopening the line had been singled and only Platform 1 was operational but, following the redoubling of the line, Platform 2 was constructed and was brought into use on 22 August 2011.

HORNBEAM PARK (HBP)

Looking north on 17 May 2016.

Hookstone Road, Harrogate, North Yorkshire HG2 8BW
SE3111153870 (53.979960, -1.5271130)
Opened 24 August 1992.
NR 2CD**HPS** 373,670

HORTON-IN-RIBBLESDALE (HIR)

Looking south on 31 May 2015. Transfers between platforms at this station are effected via a boarded level crossing at the north end.

Station Road, Horton-in-Ribblesdale, Settle, North Yorkshire
BD24 0HH
SD8036572644 (54.149240, -2.3021105)
Opened by the MR 1 May 1876 as *Horton*, renamed as *Horton-in-Ribblesdale* by the LM&SR 26 September 1927, closed by BR 4 May 1970 and reopened 14 July 1986.
NR 2**HPS** 16,112

HORWICH PARKWAY (HWI)

Looking along Platform 1 on 26 April 2016. The station is powered by green energy supplied by an adjacent wind turbine.

Arena Approach, Horwich, Bolton,
Greater Manchester BL6 6LB
SD6435109185 (53.578036, -2.5398763)
Opened 30 May 2000.
NR 2**CDHPST** 639,192

HOW WOOD (HERTS) (HWW)

Looking north on 26 May 2016.

Hyde Lane, How Wood, St Albans, Hertfordshire AL2 2JL
TL14446 03391 (51.717581, -0.34471482)
Opened 24 October 1988.
WMT 1**CDHS** 28,994

HOWWOOD (RENFREWSHIRE) (HOZ)

Station Road, Howwood, Johnstone, Renfrewshire PA9 1AZ
Location: NS39520 60458 (55.810651, -4.5624295)
Opened by the G&SWR 1 December 1876, closed by BR 7 March 1955 and reopened 12 March 2001.
ASR 2**CDHPS** 111,562

HOXTON (HOX) X

Viewed on 9 July 2016.

Geffrye Street, London E2 8FF
TQ3357983174 (51.531684, -0.075614154)
Opened 27 April 2010.
LO 2**CDHRSTTW** 2,996,342

HUCKNALL (HKN)

Looking north on 7 May 2016 with the former northbound platform, in view on the left, now a tram stop for Nottingham Express Transit trams. The original station was sited 90 yards to the north and was opened by the MR 2 October 1848 and closed 22 December 1895.

Ashgate Road, Hucknall, Nottingham NG15 7TL
SK5401849297 (53.038230, -1.1958387)
Opened by the MR 22 December 1895 as *Hucknall*, renamed as *Hucknall Byron* by BR 11 August 1952, closed 12 October 1964 and rebuilt and reopened 17 May 1993 as *Hucknall*.
EMT 1**CDHPS** 153,242

HUMPHREY PARK (HUP)

Viewed on 15 June 2016.

Chatsworth Road, Urmston, Greater Manchester M32 9QD
SJ7833795106 (53.452260, -2.3276679)
Opened 15 October 1984.
NR 2D**HS** **35,614**

HURST GREEN (HUR)

Looking along Platform 1 on 16 July 2017. The original station, *Hurst Green Halt*, was sited to the south and was opened by the LB&SCR 1 June 1907 and closed by BR 12 June 1961.

Greenhurst Lane, Hurst Green, Surrey RH8 0LL
TQ3996751402 (51.244627, 0.0039079785)
Opened 12 June 1961.
So 2CD**HPRSTTW** **634,756**

HYNDLAND (HYN)

Churchill Drive, Hyndland, Glasgow G11 7HA
NS5530067611 (55.879852, -4.3146685)
Opened 5 November 1960. The original station at Hyndland was at the end of a short branch on the north side of the line. It had been opened by the Glasgow City and District Railway 15 March 1886 and closed by BR 5 November 1960.
ASR 2CD**HRSTTW** **1,767,112**

IBM (IBM)

Looking north on 17 March 2017.

Valley Park, Inverkip Road, Inverclyde PA16 0AH
NS2348074325 (55.929497, -4.8270911)
Opened 9 May 1978 as *IBM Halt*, renamed as *IBM* 16 May 1983.
ASR 1CD**HPS** **6,032**

ILKESTON (ILN)

Looking along Platform 1 on 20 May 2017. This station is constructed on the site of *Ilkeston Junction and Cossall* which was opened by the MR on 2 May 1870 as *Ilkeston*, renamed as *Ilkeston Junction* 1 July 1890, as *Ilkeston Junction and Cossall* 1 December 1890 and closed by BR 2 January 1967.

Coronation Road, Ilkeston, Derbyshire DE7 5TE
Location: SK47430 42654 (52.979139, -1.2950617)
Funded by the Department for Transport and Derbyshire County Council with additional finance from a group of councils: Nottinghamshire County, Derbyshire County, Nottingham City, Rushcliffe Borough, Broxtowe Borough, Gedling Borough and Erewash Borough, using a Government fund designed to support infrastructure for additional housing in the Nottingham area. It was opened on 2 April 2017.
EMT 2D**HPST** **N/A**

IMBER HOUSES

Location: NG8967036611 (57.371216, -5.4996925) (Approx)
Opened 3 December 1951 as *Imeer Houses*, renamed as *Imber Houses* prior to June 1965 and closed after May 1972.

IMPERIAL COTTAGES HALT

Location: NJ2124041791 (57.459539, -3.3143869)
One of four halts opened on the Speyside route between Elgin and Aviemore on 15 June 1959, on the introduction of railbuses, and closed by the British Railways Board 18 October 1965 when services on the line were withdrawn.

IMPERIAL WHARF (IMW) X

Looking south on 6 August 2016.

Townmead Road, London SW6 2ZH
TQ2630076677 (51.474965, -0.18282200)
Opened 27 September 2009.
LO 2CD**DHS**TT 3,133,002

INSTOW

Location: SS4735830632 (51.054688, -4.1793061) (Approx)
Opened by the Bideford Extension Railway 2 November 1855, closed by BR 4 October 1965, reopened 10 January 1968 and closed 22 January 1968.

IRONBRIDGE GORGE

Location: SJ6671904097 (52.633597, -2.4931830)
Opened by the Much Wenlock, Craven Arms & Coalbrookdale Railway 1 November 1864 as *Coalbrookdale*, closed by BR 23 July 1962, reopened as *Telford (Coalbrookdale)* 27 May 1979, closed 2 September 1979, reopened as *Ironbridge Gorge* 19 July 1987 and closed 2 September 1990.

ISLIP (ISP)

Bletchingdon Road, Islip, Oxfordshire OX5 2TQ
SP5259014397 (51.825723, -1.2383249)
Opened by the Buckinghamshire Railway 1 October 1850, closed by BR 1 January 1968 and reopened as an unstaffed single platform halt 15 May 1989. The station was closed again

Looking north on 27 December 2015.

15 February 2014 to allow for a line upgrade and reopened as a two platform station 26 October 2015.
ChR 2CD**HPS** 19,600

IVYBRIDGE (IVY)

Looking west along Platform 1 on 23 May 2017. The original station, sited to the west, was opened by the South Devon Railway 15 June 1848 as *Ivy Bridge*, subsequently renamed as *Ivybridge* and closed by BR 2 March 1959.

Rutt Lane, Ivybridge, Devon PL21 0PL
SX6468556585 (50.393527, -3.9050509)
Opened 15 July 1994.
GWR 2CD**HPS** 55,518

JACKFIELD HALT

Location: SJ69214 02534 (52.619696, -2.4561659)
Opened 1 March 1954 and closed 9 September 1963.

JAMES COOK (JCH)

Marton Road, Middlesbrough TS4 3BW
NZ5130717688 (54.551847, -1.2082748)

Looking north on 26 September 2015. This station is also known as *James Cook University Hospital*.

Opened 18 May 2014.
NR 1CD**HS** 31,402

JEWELLERY QUARTER (JEQ)

Looking east on 30 March 2017. This station is also a tram stop interchange with the Midland Metro.

Vyse Street, Hockley, Birmingham B18 6LE
SP05911 87996 (52.489843, -1.9143811)
Opened 25 September 1995.
WMT 2CD**HSTT** 421,106

KELVINDALE (KVD)
Cleveden Road, Glasgow G20 0TB
NS5565369121 (55.893515, -4.3098472)
Opened 26 September 2005.
ASR 1CD**HS** 65,938

KENTISH TOWN WEST (KTW)
Prince of Wales Road, Kentish Town, Greater London NW5 3LR
TQ2859884766 (51.547139, -0.14680535)

Class 378 Unit No.378222 on Platform 1 on 4 June 2016.

Opened 1 April 1867 by the Hampstead Junction Railway as *Kentish Town,* renamed as *Kentish Town West* by the LM&SR 2 June 1924, closed by BR following a fire 18 April 1971 and reopened 5 October 1981.
LO 2C**HSTT** 2,025,772

KILMAURS (KLM)
Crofthead Road, Kilmaurs, East Ayrshire KA3 2SB
NS40812 41098 (55.637299, -4.5305541)
Opened by the Glasgow, Barrhead and Kilmarnock Joint Railway 26 June 1873, closed by BR 7 November 1966 and reopened 12 May 1984.
ASR 1CD**HPST** 104,148

KING'S CROSS THAMESLINK
Location: TQ3048382962 (51.530501, -0.12030914)
Opened by the Metropolitan Railway 10 January 1863 as *King's Cross (Met),* renamed as *King's Cross and St Pancras* in 1925, as *King's Cross St Pancras* in 1933, closed 14 May 1979, reopened 11 July 1983 as *King's Cross Midland City,* renamed as *King's Cross Thameslink* 16 May 1988 and closed 9 December 2007. The platforms are still extant.

KINGSKNOWE (KGE)
Kingsknowe Road South, Kingsknowe, Edinburgh EH14 2JR
NT2108870269 (55.919007, -3.2642081)
Opened by the CR 15 February 1848 as *Slateford,* renamed as *Kings Knowes* 1 January 1853, as *Kingsnowe* in same year, closed 1 January 1917, reopened 1 February 1919, closed by BR 6 July 1964 and reopened 1 February 1971.
ASR 2CD**HPS** 18,800

KIRKBY-IN-ASHFIELD (KKB)
Millers Way, Kirkby-in-Ashfield, Nottinghamshire NG17 8EJ
SK50102 56144 (53.100149, -1.2531696)
Opened 18 November 1996.
EMT 2C**HS** 178,808

Looking along Platform 2 on 3 May 2015.

KIRKBY STEPHEN (KSW)

Viewed on 31 May 2015.

A685, Kirkby Stephen, Cumbria CA17 4LE
NY7618506689 (54.455028, -2.3688278)
Opened by the MR 1 May 1876, renamed as *Kirkby Stephen and Ravenstonedale* 1 October 1900, as *Kirkby Stephen* by the LM&SR 1 January 1935, as *Kirkby Stephen West* by BR 8 June 1953, as *Kirkby Stephen* 6 May 1968, closed 4 May 1970 and reopened 14 July 1986.
NR 2D**HPS** 19,962

KIRK SANDALL (KKS)

Viewed on 16 April 2016.

Sandall Lane, Kirk Sandall, Doncaster, South Yorkshire DN3 1SE
SE6137507828 (53.563486, -1.0748376)
Opened 13 May 1991.
NR 2DP**S** 124,546

KIRKSTALL FORGE (KLF)

Looking along Platform 1 on 21 May 2017. The original station, sited nearby, was opened by the MR 2 July 1860 and closed 1 August 1905 when it was demolished to accommodate line widening from two to four tracks.

Abbey Road, Leeds LS5 3NF
SE2493436454 (53.823766, -1.6227123)
Opened 19 June 2016.
NR 2CD**HPS**T 94,536

KIRKWOOD (KWD)

Woodside Street, Kirkwood, Coatbridge, North Lanarkshire ML5 5NJ
NS7188864229 (55.854179, -4.0481052)
Opened 4 October 1993.
ASR 2CD**HS** 166,648

LAKE (LKE)

Looking north on 15 April 2017.

Araluen Way, Sandown, Isle of Wight PO36 8PJ
SZ5903283281 (50.646232, -1.1664350)
Opened 11 May 1987.
ILT 1D**HS** 53,786

LANDYWOOD (LAW)

Looking north along Platform 1 on 22 July 2015.

Landywood Lane, Cheslyn Hay, Walsall, Staffordshire WS6 6JE
SJ9869306549 (52.656667, -2.0207629)
Opened by the L&NWR 2 March 1908, closed 1 January 1916
and reopened by BR 10 April 1989.
WMT 2CD**HPST** 108,336

LANGHO (LHO)

Looking east towards the staggered Platform 2 on 31 May 2015.

Off Whalley New Road, Langho, Near Blackburn, Lancashire
BB6 8ED
SD7053834373 (53.804814, -2.4488421)
Opened by the Bolton, Blackburn, Clitheroe and West Yorkshire
Railway 22 June 1850, closed by BR 7 May 1956 and reopened
29 May 1994.
NR 2C**HPS** 43,996

LANGLEY MILL (LGM)

Looking north along Platform 1 on 20 May 2017 with the staggered
Platform 2 in view in the distance.

Station Road, Nottinghamshire NG16 4BP
SK4496646983 (53.018265, -1.3311495)
Opened by the MR 6 September 1847 as *Langley Mill for
Heanor*, renamed as *Langley Mill and Eastwood* 1 November
1876, as *Langley Mill and Eastwood for Heanor* by the LM&SR
11 September 1933, closed by BR 2 January 1967 and reopened
as *Langley Mill* 12 May 1986.
EMT 2**HS** 121,442

LANGWATHBY (LGW)

Viewed on 31 May 2015.

Stoney Bank, Langwathby, Near Penrith, Cumbria CA10 1NX
NY5731733474 (54.694478, -2.6637393)
Opened by the MR 1 May 1876 as *Longwathby*, renamed as
Langwathby 1 October 1876, closed by BR 4 May 1970 and
reopened 14 July 1986.
NR 2BD**HPRS** 4,132

LANGWITH-WHALEY THORNS (LAG)

Looking along Platform 2 on 3 May 2015.

Bathurst Terrace, Langwith, Derbyshire NG20 9DE
SK5287970897 (53.232486, -1.2092713)
Opened 25 May 1998.
EMT 2CD**HPS** 22,152

LARKHALL (LRH)

Caledonian Road, Larkhall, South Lanarkshire ML9 1DP
NS7609351243 (55.738672, -3.9750740)
Opened by the CR 1 July 1905 as *Larkhall Central*, renamed as *Larkhall* by BR 14 June 1965, closed 4 October 1965 and reopened 12 December 2005.
ASR 2CD**HPS**T 434,494

LAURENCEKIRK (LAU)

Station Road, Laurencekirk, Aberdeenshire AB30 1BE
NO7169771796 (56.836761, -2.4654892)
Opened by the Aberdeen Railway 1 November 1849, closed by BR 4 September 1967 and reopened 17 May 2009.
ASR 2CD**HPS**T 96,002

LAZONBY & KIRKOSWALD (LZB)

Viewed on 31 May 2015.

Seat Hill, Lazonby, Near Penrith, Cumbria CA10 1BD
NY5480239770 (54.750833, -2.7037257)
Opened by the MR as *Lazonby* 1 May 1876, renamed as *Lazonby and Kirkoswald* 1 August 1895, closed by BR 4 May 1970 and reopened 14 July 1986.
NR 2D**HS** 4,150

LEA BRIDGE (LEB)

Looking north along Platform 1 on 6 August 2017 (*Allison Smith*).

Argall Way, London E10 7PG
TQ3619287112 (51.566444, -0.036443174)
Opened by the Northern & Eastern Railway 15 September 1840 as *Lea Bridge Road*, renamed as *Lea Bridge* by the GER April 1871, closed by BR 8 July 1985 and rebuilt and reopened 16 May 2016.
AGA 2CD**HS**T 314,986

LEA GREEN (LEG)

Viewed on 11 September 2016.

Marshalls Cross Road, St Helens, Merseyside WA9 5RJ
SJ5189292453 (53.426662, -2.7254516)
Opened by the Liverpool & Manchester Railway 17 September 1830, renamed as *Sutton* in c1846 by the Grand Junction Railway, as *Lea Green* by the L&NWR June 1848, closed by BR 7 March 1955 and reopened 17 September 2000.
NR 2CD**HPS**TT 445,960

LELANT SALTINGS (LTS)

Looking south on 24 May 2017.

Saltings Reach, Lelant, St Ives, Cornwall TR27 6GH
SW5441036617 (50.178559, -5.4411922)
Opened 29 May 1978.
GWR 1CD**HPS** 121,258

LICHFIELD TRENT VALLEY (HIGH LEVEL) (LTV)

Looking north on 21 June 2015. As noted in the Introduction this is one of the stations that is combined with another (in this case *Lichfield Trent Valley Low Level*) and considered as a single entity for administration purposes by National Rail.

Trent Valley Road, Lichfield, Staffordshire WS13 6HE
SK1361909890 (52.686532, -1.7999581)
Opened by the L&NWR 3 July 1871, closed by BR 18 January 1965 and reopened 28 November 1988.
WMT 1CH**PST**TW N/A

LISVANE & THORNHILL (LVT)

Viewed on 24 May 2015.

Cherry Orchard Road, Cardiff CF14 0UE
ST1788483503 (51.544427, -3.1855443)
Opened 4 November 1985.
ATW 2CD**PST** 210,170

LIVERPOOL CENTRAL (DEEP LEVEL) (LVC) **X**

Ranelagh Street, Liverpool L1 1JT
SJ3497490174 (53.404361, -2.9795537) (Subterranean)
Opened 2 May 1977.
M 1**ABCDH**RST**TW** N/A

LIVERPOOL CENTRAL (LOW LEVEL) (LVC) **X**

Ranelagh Street, Liverpool L1 1JT
SJ3497490174 (53.404361, -2.9795537) (Subterranean)
Opened by the Mersey Railway 11 January 1892, closed by BR 28 July 1975 and reopened 2 May 1977.
M 2**ABCDH**RST**TW** N/A

LIVERPOOL LIME STREET (DEEP LEVEL) (LIV)

Lime Street, Liverpool L1 1JD
SJ3513290533 (53.407607, -2.9772440) (Subterranean)
Opened 30 October 1977.
M 1**ABCDH**PR**RST**TW N/A

LIVERPOOL SOUTH PARKWAY (LPY) **X**

Woolton Road, Garston, Liverpool L19 5PQ
SJ40888 84902 (53.357675, -2.8896216)
Opened 11 June 2006.
M 6CD**HP**R**RST**TW 1,983,726

Looking north along Platform 5 on 10 August 2016. The main line platforms are on the site of the former Allerton station, which closed 1 August 2005 to allow the required rebuilding work to commence. The Northern Line platforms (of which No.5 is one) are completely new, replacing a station at Garston which was slightly further west of the current station.

LIVINGSTON NORTH (LSN)

Deans Road North, Livingston, West Lothian EH54 8PT
NT0359168689 (55.901631, -3.5434958)
Opened 24 March 1986.
ASR 2C**DH**PS**T** 1,200,988

LIVINGSTON SOUTH (LVG)

Murieston West Road, Livingston, West Lothian EH54 9DA
NT0614565290 (55.871600, -3.5014817)
Opened 6 October 1984.
ASR 2C**DH**PS**T** 323,690

LLANFAIRPWLL (LPG)

Looking south along Platform 1 on 19 July 2015. Although contrived, this station is famed for having the longest name in Britain: *Llanfairpwllgwyngyll-gogerychwyrndrobwll-llantysilio-gogogoch*.

Holyhead Road, Llanfair PG, Anglesey LL61 5UJ
SH5259971592 (53.220867, -4.2092201)
Opened by the Chester & Holyhead Railway 1 August 1848, closed by BR 14 February 1966, reopened 29 May 1970 as a

temporary terminus following fire damage to Britannia Tubular Bridge, closed 31 January 1972 and reopened 7 May 1973.
ATW 2C**PS** 19,520

LLANHARAN (LLR)

Class 158 Unit No.158823 on Platform 2 on 2 August 2015.

Chapel Road, Llanharan, Rhondda Cynon Taff CF72 9QA
ST00090 83067 (51.537634, -3.4419313)
Opened by the GWR 1 September 1899, closed by BR 2 November 1964 and rebuilt and reopened 10 December 2007.
ATW 2C**DH**PS**T** 173,626

LLANHILLETH (LTH)

Looking south on 24 May 2015.

Commercial Road, Llanhilleth, Abertillery, Gwent NP13 2JJ
SO2169100765 (51.700142, -3.1345233)
Opened by the GWR 1 October 1901, closed by BR 30 April 1962 and reopened 27 April 2008.
ATW 1C**DH**PS**T** 87,736

LLANRWST (LWR)

Viewed on 16 July 2015.

Denbigh Street, Llanrwst, Conwy LL26 0AD
SH8004461717 (53.139059, -3.7946887)
Opened 29 July 1989.
ATW 1CD**HS** **14,770**

LLANSAMLET (LAS)

Looking along Platform 1 on 2 August 2015 with the staggered Platform 2 in view beyond the road bridge. The former GWR station, opened 1 January 1885 and closed 2 November 1964, was situated approximately 0.45 miles west of this one.

Frederick Place, Bethel Road, Llansamlet, Swansea SA7 9RY
SS6969797547 (51.661557, -3.8853045)
Opened 27 June 1994.
ATW 2CD**PS** **33,982**

LLANTWIT MAJOR (LWM)

Le Pouliguen Way, Llantwit Major, Vale of Glamorgan CF61 1ST
SS9706468889 (51.409647, -3.4814134)

Looking east along Platform 2 on 24 May 2015.

Opened by the Vale of Glamorgan Railway 1 December 1897, closed by BR 15 June 1964 and reopened 12 June 2005.
ATW 2CD**HPS**T **297,958**

LOCH AWE (LHA)

Off A85, Loch Awe, Argyle & Bute PA33 1AQ
NN1236527413 (56.401590, -5.0421801)
Opened by the Callander and Oban Railway 1 July 1880, closed by BR 1 November 1965 and reopened 1 May 1985.
ASR 1D**HPS** **4,140**

LOCH EIL OUTWARD BOUND (LHE)

Off A830, Highland PH33 7NN
NN0544278320 (56.855422, -5.1925394)
Opened 6 May 1985.
ASR 1D**HS** **572**

LOCHLUICHART (LCC)

Off A832, Lochluichart, Highland IV23 2PZ
NH3233562568 (57.621812, -4.8090452)
Opened 3 May 1954. The original station was opened as *Lochluichart High* by the Dingwall and Skye Railway on 1 July 1871. On 3 May 1954 this station was opened as *Lochluichart* as a result of a hydro-electric scheme raising the level of Loch Luichart and necessitating realignment of the line.
ASR 1D**HPS** **532**

LOCHWINNOCH (LHW)

Off A760, Lochwinnoch, Renfrewshire PA12 4JF
NS3606857962 (55.787083, -4.6159449)
Opened by the Glasgow, Paisley, Kilmarnock and Ayr Railway 12 August 1840, renamed as *Lochside* 1 June 1905, closed by BR 4 July 1955, reopened 27 June 1966 and renamed *Lochwinnoch* 13 May 1985.
ASR 2CH**PS**T **190,086**

LONDON FIELDS (LOF)

Mentmore Terrace, Hackney, London E8 3PH
TQ3478484271 (51.541251, -0.057832450)

Looking north along Platform 2 on 22 August 2017.

Opened by the GER 27 May 1872, closed 22 May 1916, reopened 1 July 1919, closed by BR 13 November 1981 and reopened 29 September 1986.
LO 2CHST **1,330,998**

LONDON ST PANCRAS INTERNATIONAL (LOW LEVEL) (STP) X

Pancras Road, London N1C 4QP
TQ3007683055 (51.531427, -0.12613310) (Subterranean)
Opened 9 December 2007.
NetR 2ABCDHPRSTTW **N/A**

LONGBECK (LGK)

Looking north along Platform 1 on 24 September 2015.

Longbeck Road, Marske-by-the-Sea, Redcar, Redcar and Cleveland TS11 6HD
NZ6271422006 (54.589369, -1.0310331)
Opened 13 May 1985.
NR 2DS **45,018**

LONGBRIDGE (LOB)

Looking south along Platform 2 on 18 July 2015. This is built on the site of the first *Longbridge* station which was opened in November 1841 by the Birmingham & Gloucester Railway and closed 1 May 1849.

Longbridge Lane, Longbridge, Birmingham B31 2TW
SP0139777644 (52.396812, -1.9808945)
Opened 8 May 1978.
WMT 2CDHSTTW **963,322**

LOSTOCK (LOT)

Looking along Platform 1 on 26 April 2016.

Rumworth Road, Lostock, Greater Manchester BL6 4JP
SD67369 08600 (53.572980, -2.4942318)
Opened c August 1852 by the Liverpool & Bury Railway as *Lostock Junction*, closed by BR 7 November 1966, reopened as *Lostock Parkway* 16 May 1988 and subsequently renamed as *Lostock*.
NR 2CDHPST **276,514**

LOSTOCK HALL (LOH)

Looking north on 31 May 2015.

Watkin Lane, Lostock Hall, Lancashire PR5 5BU
SD5475725546 (53.724342, -2.6871496)
Opened 14 May 1984.
NR 2D**HS** 39,788

LOW MOOR (LMR)

Viewed on 21 May 2017.

New Works Road, off Cleckheaton Road, Bradford,
West Yorkshire BD12 0LH
SE1641628222 (53.750110, -1.7525312)
Built by the West Yorkshire Combined Authority (WYCA),
in partnership with Network Rail, Northern and the City
of Bradford Metropolitan District Council, and opened on
2 April 2017.
NR 2C**DHPS**T **N/A**

LUIB HOUSES
Location: NH1324554716 (57.543885, -5.1221455) (Approx)
Opened 3 December 1951 and closed after 1972.

LUTON AIRPORT PARKWAY (LTN) **X**

Looking south on 30 July 2017.

Parkway Road, Luton, Bedfordshire LU1 3JW
TL1050320591 (51.872954, -0.39629638)
Opened 21 November 1999.
TL 4**AB**C**DHP**RS**TTW** 3,819,812

LYMPSTONE COMMANDO (LYC)

Looking north on 26 May 2017. When opened it was for the exclusive
use of persons with business at the adjacent Commando Training
Camp but since a dedicated footpath that passes between the camp
and the station was installed ordinary passengers are now allowed to
use it. However, the camp still possesses the key to the entrance gate
to the station and it is opened and closed as required.

Lympstone, Exmouth, Devon EX3 0PX
SX9827685722 (50.662256, -3.4406103)
Opened 3 May 1976.
GWR 1**HS** 64,690

MAENTWROG ROAD
Location: SH6942639855 (52.940159, -3.9444700)
Opened by the Bala & Ffestiniog Railway 1 November 1882, closed
by BR 4 January 1960, reopened 23 July 1989 as *Trawsffynydd* for
a Sunday tourist service and closed 10 September 1989.

MAESTEG (MST)

Looking north towards the buffer stop on 2 August 2015.

Castle Street, Maesteg, Bridgend CF34 9BL
SS8550091390 (51.609666, -3.6549255)
Opened 28 September 1992.
ATW 1C**DHPS**T 190,718

MAESTEG (EWENNY ROAD) (MEW)

Ewenny Road, Maesteg, Bridgend CF34 9TS
SS8595790888 (51.605241, -3.6481570)
Opened 26 October 1992.
ATW 1C**DHS** 3,090

MANCHESTER AIRPORT (MIA)

Malaga Avenue, Manchester M90 3RR
SJ8201785402 (53.365176, -2.2716996)
Opened 16 May 1993.
TPE 4A**B**C**DH**RR**STTW** 4,241,292

MANSFIELD (MFT)

Looking along Platform 2 on 3 May 2015.

Station Road, Mansfield, Nottinghamshire NG18 1BE
SK5370360841 (53.142018, -1.1986122)
Opened by the MR 1 March 1872, renamed by BR as *Mansfield Town* 11 August 1952, closed 12 October 1964 and reopened 20 November 1995 as *Mansfield*.
EMT 2C**DHPSTW** 399,360

MANSFIELD WOODHOUSE (MSW)

Looking north along Platform 1 on 3 May 2015.

The Sidings, Debdale Lane, Mansfield Woodhouse, Nottinghamshire NG19 7FE
SK5346763225 (53.163472, -1.2017503)
Opened by the MR 1 June 1875, closed by BR 12 October 1964 and reopened 20 November 1995.
EMT 3C**DPS** 179,602

MARLOW (MLW)

Looking towards the buffer stop on 2 July 2017. This replaced *Marlow* which was sited nearby and opened by the Great Marlow Railway 28 June 1873 as *Great Marlow*, renamed by the GWR 14 February 1899 as *Marlow* and closed by BR 10 July 1967 when the line was truncated.

Station Approach, Marlow, Buckinghamshire SL7 1NT
SU8559186521 (51.571073, -0.76641306)
Opened 10 July 1967.
GWR 1D**HPS** **276,188**

MARTINS HERON (MAO)

Looking along Platform 1 on 9 July 2017.

Whitton Road, Martins Heron, Bracknell, Berkshire RG12 9YY
SU8876368392 (51.407619, -0.72520763)
Opened 3 October 1988.
SWR 2CD**HPS**TT **586,230**

MARYHILL (MYH)

Maryhill Road, Maryhill, Glasgow G20 0BT
NS5621469551 (55.897543, -4.3011086)
Opened by the Glasgow, Dumbarton & Helensburgh Railway 31 May 1858, closed by BR 2 April 1951, reopened as *Maryhill*

Park 19 December 1960, closed to the public 2 October 1961, totally on 29 February 1964 and reopened as *Maryhill* 3 December 1993.
ASR 2CD**HS** **64,050**

MATLOCK BATH (MTB)

Looking north on 6 May 2015.

Off Dale Road, Matlock Bath, Matlock, Derbyshire DE4 3NT
SK2975158456 (53.122450, -1.5568963)
Opened by the Manchester, Buxton, Matlock & Midland Junction Railway 4 June 1849, closed by BR 6 March 1967 and reopened 27 May 1972.
EMT 1CD**HS**T **75,608**

MEADOWBANK STADIUM
Location: NT2779874495 (55.958025, -3.1580020)
Opened 14 June 1986 and closed 20 March 1989.

MEADOWHALL INTERCHANGE (MHS)

Class 144 Unit No.144010 on Platform 1 on 13 November 2012. This station is an interchange with Sheffield Supertram.

Meadowhall Road, Sheffield S9 1JQ
SK3902991296 (53.417033, -1.4142349)
Opened 5 September 1990.
NR 4CD**HP**RS**TTW** 2,015,172

MELKSHAM (MKM)

Viewed on 2 October 2015.

Station Approach, Melksham, Wiltshire SN12 8DB
ST9002864565 (51.380045, -2.1446648)
Opened by the Wiltshire, Somerset & Weymouth Railway 5 September 1848, closed by BR 18 April 1966 and reopened 13 May 1985.
GWR 1D**HP**S**T** 74,666

MELTON (SUFFOLK) (MES)

Looking north on 11 June 2017.

Wilford Bridge Road, Melton, Woodbridge, Suffolk IP12 1LT
TM2870250369 (52.104344, 1.3381138)
Opened by the East Suffolk Railway 1 June 1859, closed by BR 2 May 1955 and reopened 3 September 1984.
AGA 1B**DHP**S 68,340

MERRYTON (MEY)

Fyne Crescent, Larkhall, South Lanarkshire ML9 2UW
NS7596952394 (55.748978, -3.9775738)
Opened 12 December 2005.
ASR 1CD**HP**S 123,066

METHERINGHAM (MGM)

Viewed on 2 April 2016.

Station Road, Metheringham, Lincolnshire LN4 3HD
TF0771561413 (53.138996, -0.39122432)
Opened 1 August 1882 by the Great Northern & Great Eastern Joint Railway as *Blankney and Metheringham*, closed by BR 11 September 1961 and reopened as *Metheringham* on 6 October 1975.
EMT 2D**HP**S 99,704

METROCENTRE (MCE)

Looking east along Platform 2 on 25 September 2015.

Gateshead Metro Centre, Gateshead, Tyne and Wear NE11 9GA
NZ2154862750 (54.958928, -1.6650349)
Opened 3 August 1987 as *Gateshead MetroCentre* and renamed as *MetroCentre* 17 May 1993.
NR 2CD**H**S 350,376

MILLIKEN PARK (MIN)
Cochranemill Road, Milliken Park, Renfrewshire PA5 0NU
NS4134061969 (55.824813, -4.5342931)
Opened 15 May 1989.
ASR 2CD**HS 241,398**

MILLS HILL (MANCHESTER) (MIH)

Class 150 Unit No.150268 departing from the station on 28 June 2015.

Oldham Road, Middleton, Greater Manchester M24 2EH
SD8873506077 (53.551202, -2.1715003)
Opened by the Manchester and Leeds Railway 4 July 1839, closed
11 August 1842 and rebuilt and reopened by BR 25 March 1985.
NR 2C**PS**T **330,628**

MILTON KEYNES CENTRAL (MKC) **X**

Looking north along Platform 2 on 10 November 2016.

302 Eldergate, Milton Keynes Central, Milton Keynes MK9 1LA
SP84174 37994 (52.033977, -0.77436715)
Opened 14 May 1982.
WMT 5AB**CD**H**PR**R**STTW 6,851,324**

MITCHAM EASTFIELDS (MTC)

Looking north along Platform 2 on 23 July 2016 with the staggered
Platform 1 visible beyond the level crossing.

Eastfields Road, Mitcham, Greater London CR4 2ND
TQ2845169269 (51.407907, -0.15455157)
Opened 2 June 2008.
So 2C**DHS**TTW **1,379,508**

MONKS RISBOROUGH (MRS)

Viewed on 2 July 2017, this station replaced the original one opened by
the GWR 11 November 1929 as *Monks Risborough and Whiteleaf Halt*,
renamed by BR as *Monks Risborough and Whiteleaf* 5 May 1969, as *Monks
Risborough* 6 May 1974 and closed 13 January 1986.

Crowbrook Road, Monks Risborough, Buckinghamshire
HP27 9LW
SP8094404787 (51.735956, -0.82922369)
Opened 13 January 1986.
ChR 1C**DH**ST **19,952**

MOORFIELDS (DEEP LEVEL) (MRF) **X**
Moorfields, Liverpool L2 2BS
SJ3437490624 (53.408331, -2.9886709) (Subterranean)
Opened 8 May 1978.
M 1B**CDH**R**STTW N/A**

MOORFIELDS (LOW LEVEL) (MRF) X

Moorfields, Liverpool L2 2BS
SJ3437490624 (53.408331, -2.9886709) (Subterranean)
Opened 2 May 1977.
M 2BCDHRSTTW N/A

MOORGATE (MOG) X

Moorfields, London EC2Y 9AE
TQ3269781683 (51.518489, -0.088879019) (Subterranean)
Opened by the Great Northern and City Railway 14 February 1904, closed by the LTE 1 March 1975 and reopened by BR 8 November 1976.
GN 2ABCHSTT 10,833,978

MORECAMBE (MCM)

Looking south on 8 April 2017.

Looking west towards the head shunt on 20 September 2015. This replaced the second station here, opened by the MR 24 March 1907 as *Morecambe*, renamed by the LM&SR 2 June 1924 as *Morecambe Promenade*, by BR 6 May 1968 as *Morecambe* and closed 7 February 1994 when the line was truncated.

Central Drive, Morecambe, Lancashire LA4 4BL
SD4324264163 (54.070262, -2.8688116)
Opened 6 June 1994.
NR 2DHPST 237,976

MOSSPARK (MPK)

Dundee Drive, Mosspark, Glasgow G52 3RN
NS5310563320 (55.840669, -4.3474035)
Opened by LM&SR 1 March 1934 as *Mosspark West*, renamed by BR as *Mosspark* 3 May 1976, closed 10 January 1983 and reopened 30 July 1990.
ASR 1CDHS 186,728

MOSS SIDE (MOS)

Lytham Road, Moss Side, Lancashire FY8 4NB
SD3794030247 (53.764860, -2.9429278)
Opened by the Preston and Wyre Joint Railway in 1847, closed by BR 26 June 1961 and reopened 21 November 1983.
NR 1DHS 2,828

MOULSECOOMB (MCB)

Looking along Platform 1 on 2 October 2016.

Queensdown School Road, Moulsecoomb, Brighton, East Sussex BN2 4GP
TQ3254106945 (50.846852, -0.11867970)
Opened 12 May 1980.
So 2CHSTT 332,108

MOUNTAIN ASH (MTA)

Viewed on 10 March 2015.

Henry Street, Mountain Ash,
Rhondda Cynon Taff CF45 3HD
ST0493898997 (51.681660, -3.3763781)
Opened 29 January 2001.
ATW 2C**DHPS** 93,664

MOUNT VERNON (MTV)
Hamilton Road, Mount Vernon, Glasgow G32 9RD
NS6652162856 (55.840398, -4.1331097)
Opened by the Rutherglen and Coatbridge Railway 8 January
1866, closed by the LM&SR 16 August 1943 and reopened by
BR 4 October 1993.
ASR 2CD**HS** 66,828

MUIR OF ORD (MOO)
Corry Road, Muir of Ord, Highland IV6 7QJ
NH5274550127 (57.517292, -4.4601434)
Opened by the Inverness & Ross-shire Railway 11 June 1862,
closed by BR 13 June 1960 and reopened 4 October 1976.
ASR 2**HPS** 64,480

MUSSELBURGH (MUB)
Whitehill Farm Road, Musselburgh, East Lothian EH21 6TR
NT3309271679 (55.933499, 55.933499)
Opened 3 October 1988.
ASR 2CD**HPST** 463,690

NARBOROUGH (NBR)

Looking east along Platform 1 on 1 September 2015.

Station Road, Narborough, Leicestershire LE19 2HR
SP5408797337 (52.571179, -1.2033865)
Opened by the South Leicestershire Railway 1 January 1864,
closed by BR 4 March 1968 and reopened 5 January 1970.
EMT 2CD**HPSST** 397,674

NEEDHAM MARKET (NMT)

Looking along Platform 1 on 11 June 2017.

Station Yard, Needham Market, Ipswich IP6 8AS
TM0912854881 (52.152589, 1.0555270)
Opened by the Ipswich, Bury & Norwich Railway 24 December
1846 as *Needham*, closed by BR 2 January 1967 and reopened
6 December 1971 as *Needham Market*.
AGA 2C**HPS** 91,706

NEWBRIDGE (NBE)

Viewed on 24 May 2015.

Off Bridge Street, Newbridge, Caerphilly NP11 5FH
ST2103196906 (51.665365, -3.1431922)
Opened by the Monmouthshire Railway 23 December
1850, closed by BR 30 April 1962 and rebuilt and reopened
6 February 2008.
ATW 1CD**HPST** 135,866

NEWCOURT (NCO)

Viewed on 25 May 2017.

Station Road, Exeter, Devon EX2 7FR
SX96103 90253 (50.702601, -3.4726211)
Opened 4 June 2015.
GWR 1CDST 99,394

NEWCRAIGHALL (NEW)

Off Newcraighall Road, Newcraighall, Musselburgh EH21 8QT
NT3195071646 (55.933043, -3.0908006)
Opened 3 June 2002.
ASR 1CDHPST 234,770

NEW CUMNOCK (NCK)

Pathbrae, New Cumnock, East Ayrshire KA18 4DF
NS6185414205 (55.402261, -4.1831464)
Opened by the Glasgow, Paisley, Kilmarnock and Ayr Railway 20 May 1850, closed by BR 6 December 1965 and reopened 27 May 1991.
ASR 2CDHPS 26,604

NEW HOLLAND (NHL)

Looking west on 17 April 2016.

Lincoln Castle Way, New Holland, Barrow-upon-Humber, North Lincolnshire DN19 7RR
TA0835424089 (53.701997, -0.36015362)
Opened 24 June 1981.
NR 1DPS 14,996

NEWICK AND CHAILEY

Location: TQ4007921058 (50.971907, -0.0062602758)
Opened by the Lewes & East Grinstead Railway 1 August 1882, closed by BR 30 May 1955, reopened 7 August 1956 and closed 17 March 1958.

NEW PUDSEY (NPD)

Class 144 Unit No.144019 on Platform 1 on 18 June 2016.

Owlcotes Lane, Stanningley, Pudsey, West Yorkshire LS28 6QG
SE2113534311 (53.804668, -1.6805622)
Opened 6 March 1967.
NR 2CDHPRSTTW 901,862

NEWSTEAD (NSD)

Looking north on 7 May 2016.

Station Road, Newstead, Nottinghamshire NG15 0BZ
SK5223152821 (53.070080, -1.2219205)
Opened 17 May 1993.
EMT 1CDPS 35,868

NEWTON AYCLIFFE (NAY)

Looking north along Platform 1 on 25 September 2015.

Greenfield Way, Newton Aycliffe, Durham DL5 7BD
NZ2658724368 (54.613775, -1.5898499)
Opened 9 January 1978.
NR 2CD**HPS** 61,944

NEWTONGRANGE (NEG)

23 Murderdean Road, Newtongrange EH22 4PE
NT3319364199 (55.866318, -3.0690560)
Opened by the NBR 1 August 1908, closed by BR 6 January 1969 and rebuilt and reopened 6 September 2015.
ASR 1CD**HPS**T 141,644

NEWTOWN HALT

Location: TG5284909022 (52.620038, 1.7341098)
Opened by the M&GN on 17 July 1933, closed September 1939, reopened by BR June 1948 and closed 2 March 1959.

NINIAN PARK (NNP)

Looking east on 24 May 2015 with Cardiff Canton Depot in view in the distance.

Leckwith Road, Cardiff CF11 8HP
ST1665375975 (51.476572, -3.2015088)
Opened by the GWR 2 November 1912 as *Ninian Park Platform*, initially for matchday traffic only until c1934. Closed 3 September 1939, reopened by BR for football traffic c1970 as *Ninian Park*, closed c1976 and reopened for regular passenger use 4 October 1987.
ATW 2CD**ST** 125,622

NOTTINGHAM ARKWRIGHT STREET

Location: SK5719538215 (52.938292, -1.1504232)
Opened by the GCR on 15 March 1899 as *Arkwright Street*, renamed as *Nottingham Arkwright Street* 24 May 1900, closed by BR 4 March 1963, reopened 4 September 1967 and closed 5 May 1969.

OKEHAMPTON (OKE)

Looking north on 23 May 2017. This station has been restored and is owned by the Dartmoor Railway heritage line with the Great Western Railway TOC running occasional trains on summer weekends.

Station Road, Okehampton, Devon EX20 1EJ
SX5922794430 (50.732381, -3.9961132)
Opened by the Devon & Cornwall Railway 3 October 1871, closed by BR 5 June 1972 and reopened 25 May 1997.
GWR 2**BRSTW** 5,926

OLD STREET (OLD) X

Old Street, London EC1Y 1BE
TQ3276582501 (51.525827, -0.087598264) (Subterranean)
Opened by the Great Northern and City Railway 14 February 1904, closed by the LPTE 5 October 1975 and reopened by BR 16 August 1976.
GN 2A**CHRSTW** 5,323,546

ORESTON

Location: SX5044453376 (50.361243, -4.1039929) (Approx)
Opened by the L&SWR 1 January 1897, closed by BR 15 January 1951, reopened 2 July 1951 and closed 10 September 1951.

OUTWOOD (OUT)

Looking along Platform 2 on 7 May 2016. An earlier station, sited on the opposite side of the bridge in view in the distance, was opened by the Bradford, Wakefield & Leeds Railway in 1858 as *Lofthouse*, renamed as *Lofthouse and Outwood* by the GNR July 1865 and closed by BR 13 June 1960.

Lingwell Court, Outwood, Wakefield, West Yorkshire WF3 3HR
SE3241124456 (53.715520, -1.5103760)
Opened 12 July 1988.
NR 2CD**HPS** 407,166

OVERPOOL (OVE)

Viewed on 17 May 2015.

Overpool Lane, Ellesmere Port, Cheshire CH66 3NP
SJ3843476746 (53.284097, -2.9249033)
Opened 15 August 1988.
M 2C**HST** 154,966

OXFORD PARKWAY (OXP) **X**

Water Eaton Park & Ride, Oxford Road,
Oxford OX2 8HA
SP5012511996 (51.804362, -1.2744382)
Opened 25 October 2015.
ChR 2AC**DHPRSTW** 809,812

Looking south on 27 December 2015.

PAISLEY CANAL (PCN)

Causeyside Street, Paisley, Renfrewshire PA1 1TU
NS4837063432 (55.840205, -4.4230083)
Opened 28 July 1990. The original station was opened by the G&SWR 1 July 1885, closed by BR 10 January 1983 and the site sold off. When passenger services were reinstated the new station was constructed to the east of the original one.
ASR 1D**HST** 398,148

PARK LEAZE HALT

Location: SU0063898750 (51.687507, -1.9921651)
Opened 4 January 1960 and closed 6 April 1964.

PARTICK (PTK)

Merkland Street, Partick, Glasgow G11 6BU
NS5560866478 (55.869770, -4.3091431)
Opened 17 December 1979. This replaced *Partick* which was opened by the NBR 1 December 1882, renamed by BR 28 February 1953 as *Partick Hill* and closed 17 December 1979 when it was re-sited to provide an interchange with Glasgow Subway.
ASR 2AB**C**DH**RSTW** 3,026,006

PEARTREE (PEA)

Class 153 Unit No. 153321 departing south on 30 April 2016. This station is unique inasmuch as it has electronic gates and access by passengers is only gained via an intercom system just prior to the arrival of a train.

Osmaston Park Road, Peartree, Derby DE24 8DT
SK3557933458 (52.897396, -1.4725596)
Opened by the Birmingham & Derby Junction Railway 12 August 1839 as *Pear Tree and Normanton*, closed by BR 4 March 1968 and reopened as *Peartree* 4 October 1976.
EMT 2D**H**SS **4,132**

PENALLY (PNA)

Looking west on 14 June 2017.

Off A4139, Penally, Tenby, Pembrokeshire SA70 7PS
SS1180999061 (51.658744, -4.7222087)
Opened by the Pembroke & Tenby Railway in October 1863, closed by BR 15 June 1964, reopened 29 June 1970, closed 16 November 1970, reopened 5 April 1971, closed 13 September 1971 and reopened 28 February 1972.
ATW 1D**H**PSW **5,332**

PENCOED (PCD)

Viewed on 2 August 2015.

Hendre Road, Pencoed, Bridgend CF35 6TA
SS9593581632 (51.523985, -3.5013905)
Opened by the South Wales Railway 2 September 1850, closed by BR 2 November 1964 and reopened 11 May 1992.
ATW 2CD**H**ST **233,420**

PENRHIWCEIBER (PER)

Looking north on 10 May 2015 with the degraded former southbound platform in view on the right.

Station Terrace, Penrhiwceiber, Rhondda Cynon Taff CF45 3ST
ST0604297693 (51.670127, -3.3600703)
Opened by the Aberdare Railway 6 August 1846, renamed as *Penrhiwceiber Low Level* by the GWR 1 July 1924, closed by BR October 1980 and reopened as *Penrhiwceiber* 3 October 1988.
ATW 1CD**H**S **44,000**

PINHOE (PIN)

Looking east along Platform 2 on 25 May 2017.

Pinn Lane, Pinhoe, Devon EX1 3SB
SX9632594166 (50.737820, -3.4705827)
Opened by the L&SWR 30 October 1871, closed by BR 7 March 1966 and reopened 16 May 1983.
SWR 2CD**H**ST **121,342**

PITTENZIE HALT
Location: NN8683120800 (56.365928, -3.8335580)
Opened 15 September 1958, closed 6 July 1964.

POLEGATE (PLG) **X**

Looking along Platform 1 on 2 October 2016. This station is built on the site of the first which was opened by the LB&SCR 27 June 1846 and closed 3 October 1881.

High Street, Polegate, East Sussex BN26 6AN
TQ5831004804 (50.821143, 0.24615437)
Opened 25 May 1986.
So 2**BCDHPST**T**W** **850,722**

PONTEFRACT TANSHELF (POT)

Looking along Platform 2 on 7 May 2016.

Beechnut Lane, Pontefract, West Yorkshire WF8 4RG
SE4508722177 (53.694102, -1.3186651)
Opened by the L&YR 17 July 1871 as *Tanshelf*, renamed as *Pontefract Tanshelf* by the LM&SR 1 December 1936, closed by BR 2 January 1967 and reopened 11 May 1992.
NR 2**DPS** **33,328**

PONTYCLUN (PYC)

Station Approach, Pontyclun, Bridgend CF72 9DS
ST0352181468 (51.523855, -3.3920422)

Viewed on 2 August 2015.

A joint station opened by the South Wales Railway 18 June 1850 and the Cowbridge Railway 18 September 1865 as *Llantrissant*, amalgamated by the GWR 1925, closed by BR 2 November 1964 and reopened as *Pontyclun* 28 September 1992.
ATW 2**CDHPS**T **302,896**

PORTISHEAD

Location: ST4717576478 (51.484777, -2.7621549) (Approx)
Opened 4 January 1954 and closed 7 September 1964.

PORTLETHEN (PLN)

Class 170 No.170413 on a service to Aberdeen on 18 September 2015.

Cookston Road, Portlethen, Aberdeenshire AB12 4JS
NO9233196702 (57.061305, -2.1280727)
Opened by the Aberdeen Railway 1 February 1850, closed by BR 11 June 1956 and reopened 17 May 1985.
ASR 2**DHPS**T **45,936**

POSSILPARK & PARKHOUSE (PPK)
Balmore Road, Glasgow G22 6LN
NS5886468639 (55.890135, -4.2582884)
Opened 3 December 1993.
ASR 2CD**HS** 73,138

POTTER HEIGHAM BRIDGE HALT
Location:TG4207318578 (52.710676, 1.5822592)
Opened by the M&GN 17 July 1933, closed September 1939, reopened by BR June 1948 and closed 2 March 1959.

POYLE ESTATE HALT
Location:TQ0360076200 (51.475286, -0.50968275)
Opened 4 January 1954 and closed 29 March 1965.

PRESTWICK INTERNATIONAL AIRPORT (PRA)
International Airport, Rail Station, Prestwick, South Ayrshire
KA9 1NY
NS3501327032 (55.509109, -4.6141773)
Opened 5 September 1994 as *Glasgow Prestwick Airport* and subsequently renamed as *Prestwick International Airport.*
ASR 2D**HPSW** 117,870

PRIESTHILL & DARNLEY (PTL)
Kennishead Road, Glasgow G53 6UL
NS5327560126 (55.812045, -4.3429698)
Opened 23 April 1990.
ASR 2CD**HS** 144,766

PYE CORNER (PYE)

Looking south on 24 May 2015.

Western Valley Road, Pye Corner,
Newport NP10 9DT
ST2794187461 (51.581380, -3.0413595)
Opened 14 December 2014.
ATW 1CD**HPS**T 81,342

PYLE (PYL)
Beach Road, Pyle, Bridgend CF33 6AR
SS82343 82075 (51.525293, -3.6973742)
Opened 27 June 1994.
ATW 2D**HPS** 118,910

RADCLIVE HALT
Location: SP6786834078 (52.001000, -1.0127994)
Opened 13 August 1956 and closed 2 January 1961.

RAMSGREAVE & WILPSHIRE (RGW)
Ramsgreave Road, Wilpshire, Lancashire BB1 9BH
SD6859431622 (53.779976, -2.4780741)
Opened 29 May 1994.
NR 2C**HPS** 113,542

RAMSLINE HALT
Location: SK36067 34339 (52.905278, -1.4652023)
Opened 20 January 1990 as *Baseball Ground Halt*, for football traffic and only used four times, all in the first season. Closed 1997 and still extant in 2016.

REDCAR BRITISH STEEL (RBS)

Looking north on 24 September 2015, this station is within the former SSI Steel Complex and is not accessible for public use. Sadly, the exit and entry total of just 50 reflects the loss of employment following the closure of most of the plant in 2015.

SSI Steel Complex, Trunk Road, Redcar,
Redcar and Cleveland TS10 5QW
NZ5742024208 (54.609780, -1.1125079)
Opened 19 June 1978.
NR 2**HS** 50

REDDITCH (RDC)
Bromsgrove Road, Redditch, Worcestershire B97 4RB
SP0379567636 (52.306826, -1.9457683)
Opened 7 February 1972.
WMT 1BCD**HPS**TT 1,032,940

Class 323 Unit No.323209 at the buffer stops on 22 October 2016. Following the closure of the line south of Redditch on 17 June 1963 the second station, which had been opened by the MR 4 May 1868, continued in use until this one, sited further north, was opened, allowing demolition of the station for development of a bus station and car park.

RETFORD (LOW LEVEL) (RET)

Looking east on 17 April 2016. Although technically part of Retford station, the opening of this low-level station relieved the bottle neck, and speed restrictions, created by the level crossing of the East Coast Main Line and the Worksop to Gainsborough line.

Station Road, Retford, Nottinghamshire DN22 7DE
SK7040280181 (53.313891, -0.94475448)
Opened 14 June 1965.
VTEC 2CD**HP**R**STTW N/A**

RHOOSE CARDIFF INTERNATIONAL AIRPORT (RIA)

Off Torbay Terrace, Rhoose, Vale of Glamorgan CF62 3HB
ST0620766214 (51.387189, -3.3492824)
Opened by the Barry Railway 1 December 1897 as *Rhoose*, closed by BR 15 June 1964 and reopened as *Rhoose Cardiff International Airport* 12 June 2005.
ATW 2CD**HPS**T 181,272

Looking east along Platform 1 on 24 May 2015. This currently has the longest official station name on the National Rail system.

RHU HALT
Location: NS2722484463 (56.021831, -4.7737379)
Opened by the West Highland Railway on 7 August 1894 as *Row*, renamed as *Rhu* by the L&NER 24 February 1927, closed by BR 9 January 1956, reopened 4 April 1960 as *Rhu Halt* and closed 15 June 1964.

RIBBLEHEAD (RHD)

Looking south along Platform 1 on 31 May 2015 with the staggered Platform 2, which can only be accessed by a boarded level crossing, in view in the distance.

Low Sleights Road, Chapel Le Dale, North Yorkshire LA6 3JF
SD7660978918 (54.205466, -2.3601052)
Opened by the MR 4 December 1876 as *Batty Green*, renamed as *Ribblehead* 1 May 1877, closed by BR 4 May 1970 and reopened 14 July 1986.
NR 2P**S** 17,734

RISCA & PONTYMISTER (RCA)

Looking north along Platform 1 on 24 May 2015.

Off Maryland Road, Risca, Caerphilly NP11 6BD
ST2446890229 (51.605814, -3.0920640)
Opened 6 February 2008.
ATW 2CD**HPS**T 111,344

ROCHESTER (RTR) **X**

Looking east along Platform 2 on 1 May 2017. This replaced the original one, sited 560 yards to the east and opened by the London, Chatham and Dover Railway 1 March 1892 and closed by BR 13 December 2015.

Corporation Street, Rochester, Kent ME1 1NH
TQ7454368563 (51.389265, 0.50721109)
Opened 13 December 2015.
So 3B**CDHS**TTW 1,631,718

ROGART (ROG)

Off A839, Rogart, Highland IV28 3XA
NC7247801981 (57.988710, -4.1585585)
Opened by the Sutherland Railway 13 April 1868, closed by BR 13 June 1960, reopened 6 March 1961, renamed as *Rogart Halt* 12 June 1961 and renamed as *Rogart* 17 May 1982.
ASR 2D**HPS** 1,948

ROGERSTONE (ROR)

Looking north on 24 May 2015.

Lily Way, Afon Village, Rogerstone, Newport NP10 9LG
ST2624589044 (51.595392, -3.0661646)
Opened 6 February 2008.
ATW 1CD**HPS**T 90,088

ROTHERHAM CENTRAL (RMC)

Class 158 Unit No.158797 on Platform 2 on 16 April 2016.

Central Road, Rotherham, South Yorkshire S60 1QH
SK4257193002 (53.432092, -1.3607195)
Opened by the Manchester, Sheffield and Lincolnshire Railway 1 February 1874 as *Rotherham*, renamed 1886/7 as *Rotherham and Masborough*, as *Rotherham Central* by BR 25 September 1950, closed 5 September 1966 and rebuilt and reopened 11 May 1987.
NR 2C**DHPRS**TW 690,734

ROUGHTON ROAD (RNR)

Looking west on 18 June 2017.

Roughton Road, Cromer, Norfolk NR27 9LN
TG2194740709 (52.917918, 1.2998883)
Opened 20 May 1985.
AGA 1**HS** 15,998

RUGELEY TOWN (RGT)

Looking north along Platform 1 on 23 August 2015.

Wharf Road, Rugeley, Staffordshire WS15 1BL
SK0434917450 (52.754646, -1.9370002)
Opened by the L&NWR 1 June 1870, closed by BR 18 January
1965 and reopened 2 June 1997.
WMT 2C**DHPS** 141,844

RUNCORN EAST (RUE)

Barnfield Avenue, Runcorn, Cheshire WA7 6RW
SJ5576481422 (53.327852, -2.6656410)
Opened 3 October 1983.
ATW 2C**DHPS**TT 183,306

Looking along Platform 2 on 17 May 2015.

RUSKINGTON (RKT)

Viewed on 2 April 2016.

Station Road, Ruskington, Sleaford, Lincolnshire NG34 9FS
TF0867950573 (53.041397, -0.38047403)
Opened by the Great Northern & Great Eastern Joint Railway
6 March 1882, closed by BR 11 September 1961 and reopened
5 May 1975.
EMT 2D**HPS** 91,016

RUTHERGLEN (RUT)

Farmeloan Road, Rutherglen, South Lanarkshire G73 1LX
NS6150061934 (55.830704, -4.2127472)
Opened 5 November 1979 and replaced the original station,
sited nearby, which had been opened by the CR 31 March 1879.
ASR 2C**DHS**TT 1,098,300

RYDER BROW (RRB)

Viewed on 19 May 2016.

Levenshulme Road, Reddish, Greater Manchester M18 7PR
SJ8856695578 (53.456825, -2.1736649)
Opened 4 November 1985.
NR 2**HS** 30,266

ST MICHAELS (STM)

Southwood Road, Liverpool L17 7BQ
SJ3669886964 (53.375719, -2.9529861)
Opened by the Garston and Liverpool Railway 1 June 1864,
closed by BR 17 April 1972 and reopened 3 January 1978.
M 2**CH**P**RST** 1,006,394

SALFORD CRESCENT (SLD) X

University Road West, Salford, Greater Manchester M5 4BR
SJ8179898882 (53.486334, -2.2757778)
Opened 11 May 1987.
NR 2**CDHSTTW** 1,148,814

SALTAIRE (SAE)

Looking along Platform 2 on 18 June 2016.

Victoria Road, Bradford BD18 4PS
SE1386638058 (53.838589, -1.7907661)
Opened by the MR 1 May 1856, closed by BR 22 March 1965
and reopened 9 April 1984.
NR 2**DST** 913,154

SAMPFORD COURTENAY (SMC)

Looking north on 23 May 2017. Totally devoid of facilities and locked
up when not in use, this station is owned by the Dartmoor Railway
heritage line and the Great Western Railway TOC runs occasional
trains on summer weekends.

Belstone Corner, Okehampton, Devon EX20 2SP
SX62662 98540 (50.770146, -3.9490029)
Opened by the Devon & Cornwall Railway 8 January 1867 as
Okehampton Road, renamed as *Belstone Corner* 3 October 1871,
as *Sampford Courtenay* 1 January 1872, as *Sampford Courtenay
Halt* by BR 12 September 1965, as *Sampford Courtenay* 5 May
1969, closed 5 June 1972 and reopened 23 May 2004.
GWR 1 144

SANDAL & AGBRIGG (SNA)

Looking along Platform 2 on 7 May 2016.

Agbrigg Road, Sandal, Wakefield, West Yorkshire WF2 6AA
SE3438318630 (53.663033, -1.4811534)
Opened by the West Riding & Grimsby Railway 1 February
1866 as *Sandal*, closed by BR 4 November 1957 and reopened
30 November 1987 as *Sandal and Agbrigg*.
NR 2**CHPST** 281,450

SANQUHAR (SQH)

Station Road, Sanquhar, Dumfries and Galloway DG4 6BS
NS7811110255 (55.371106, -3.9248577)
Opened by the Glasgow, Paisley, Kilmarnock and Ayr Railway
28 October 1850, closed by BR 6 December 1965 and reopened
27 June 1994.
ASR 2**CDHPS** 27,350

SARN (SRR)

Heol Persondy, Off Sarn Hill, Sarn, Bridgend CF32 9RL
SS8984383406 (51.538768, -3.5897318)
Opened 28 September 1992.
ATW 1**CDPS** 60,192

SCALE HALL

Location: SD4618562549 (54.056072, -2.8235695) (Approx)
Opened 8 June 1957 and closed 3 January 1966.

SCRATBY HALT

Location: TG5089914801 (52.672778, 1.7097420) (Approx)
Opened by the M&GN 17 July 1933, closed September 1939,
reopened by BR June 1948 and closed 2 March 1959.

SHAWFAIR (SFI)

9 Harelaw, Dalkeith, Midlothian EH22 1SB
NT3196069916 (55.917500, -3.0902000)
Opened 6 September 2015.
ASR 2CD**HPS**T **22,236**

SHEPHERD'S BUSH (SPB) **X**

Looking north on 6 August 2016, this is partially built on the site of the West London Railway station that opened 27 May 1844 and closed 1 December 1844 and Uxbridge Road which was opened by the West London Railway 1 November 1869 and closed 21 October 1940.

Holland Park Roundabout, *Uxbridge Road*, Shepherds Bush, London W12 8LB
TQ2378280034 (51.505694, -0.21788388)
Opened 28 September 2008.
LO 2A**C**D**H**R**ST**T **7,984,042**

SHERBURN-IN-ELMET (SIE)

Looking along Platform 1 on 17 May 2016.

Oak Terrace, Sherburn-in-Elmet, Near Selby, North Yorkshire LS25 6DY
SE5062533721 (53.797343, -1.2329122)

Opened by the York & North Midland Railway 30 May 1839 as *Sherburn*, renamed as *Sherburn-in-Elmet* by the NER 1 July 1903, closed by BR 13 September 1965 and reopened 9 July 1984.
NR 2D**HPS** **47,488**

SHERINGHAM (SHM)

Looking west on 18 June 2017 with the signal box and station of the North Norfolk heritage railway in view beyond the level crossing.

Station Road, Sheringham, Norfolk NR26 8RA
TG1581843055 (52.941468, 1.2104461)
Opened 2 January 1967.
AGA 1CD**HPS** **209,952**

SHIELDMUIR (SDM)

John Street, Shieldmuir, North Lanarkshire ML2 7TF
NS7729855524 (55.777418, -3.9578167)
Opened 14 May 1990.
ASR 2CD**HS** **113,940**

SHIREBROOK (SHB)

Looking along Platform 2 on 3 May 2015.

Station Road, Shirebrook, Derbyshire NG20 8SX
SK5335967745 (53.204111, -1.2026033)

Opened by the MR 1 June 1875, renamed as *Shirebrook West* by BR 18 June 1951, closed 12 October 1964 and reopened 25 May 1998 as *Shirebrook*.
EMT 2D**HPS 84,848**

SHOREDITCH HIGH STREET (SDC) **X**
Braithwaite Street, London E1 6GJ
TQ3363382241 (51.523287, -0.075195730)
Opened 27 April 2010. This is built on the site of *Shoreditch* station which was opened by the Eastern Counties Railway 1 July 1840, renamed as *Bishopsgate* by the GER 27 July 1846 and closed 1 November 1875.
LO 2C**DH**R**STT 7,855,004**

SHOTTON (LOW LEVEL) (SHT)

Looking west along Platform 2 on 17 May 2015. Along with *Shotton High Level*, which was opened by the Wrexham, Mold and Connah's Quay Railway 1 October 1891, these two stations are considered to be one - *Shotton* - by National Rail.

Chester Road West, Shotton, Flintshire CH5 1BX
SJ3079069051 (53.213990, -3.0378565)
Opened by the L&NWR in 1907, renamed as *Shotton Low Level* by BR 15 September 1952, closed 14 February 1966 and reopened as *Shotton* 21 August 1972.
ATW 2**PST N/A**

SILEBY (SIL)

Looking north on 15 August 2015.

King Street, Sileby, Leicestershire LE12 7UW
SK6023015211 (52.731189, -1.1095092)
Opened by the Midland Counties Railway 5 May 1840, closed by BR 4 March 1968 and reopened 28 May 1994.
EMT 2C**HPS 116,452**

SILKSTONE COMMON (SLK)

Viewed on 7 May 2016.

Knabbs Lane, Silkstone Common, Barnsley, South Yorkshire S75 4RB
SE2900704335 (53.534875, -1.5638191)
Opened by the Manchester, Sheffield and Lincolnshire Railway 1 July 1854 as *Silkstone*, closed by BR 29 June 1959 and reopened as *Silkstone Common* 26 November 1984.
NR 1**HPS 40,248**

SINFIN CENTRAL
Location: SK3578532356 (52.887474, -1.469616)
Opened 4 October 1976 and closed 17 May 1998 – officially on 23 September 2002.

SINFIN NORTH
Location: SK3536332940 (52.892754, -1.475828)
Opened 4 October 1976 and closed 17 May 1993 – officially on 23 September 2002.

SKEWEN (SKE)

Looking along Platform 2 on 2 August 2015.

Station Road, Skewen, Neath SA10 6HF
SS7233497462 (51.661399, -3.8471755)
Opened by the GWR 1 May 1910, closed by BR 2 November 1964 and reopened 27 June 1994.
ATW 2CD**HPS** 43,180

SLAITHWAITE (SWT)

Looking along Platform 2 on 15 May 2016 with the staggered Platform 1 in view in the distance. This station is partially sited on the previous one, opened by the Huddersfield & Manchester Railway 1 August 1849 and closed by BR 7 October 1968.

Station Road, Kirklees, West Yorkshire HD7 5EE
SE0793514152 (53.623848, -1.8815026)
Opened 13 December 1982.
NR 2D**HPST** 204,946

SMALLBROOK JUNCTION (SAB)

Class 483 Unit No.483004 on a service to Ryde Pier Head. This station is unique in that there is no access by public road and it acts as an interchange between a heritage line, the Isle of Wight Steam Railway, and a national rail network, Island Line Trains.

Smallbrook Lane, Smallbrook, Isle of Wight PO33 1AZ
SZ5974990552 (50.711535, -1.1551282)
Opened 21 July 1991.
ILT 2D**HS** 12,768

SMETHWICK GALTON BRIDGE (SGB)

Class 172 Unit No.172338 on Platform 1 on 27 June 2015. This station is built on two levels with the Birmingham Snow Hill to Stourbridge line on the high level (Platforms 1 and 2) and the Birmingham New Street to Wolverhampton (Platforms 3 and 4) on the low.

Galton Bridge, Warley, West Midlands B66 1HU
SP0142789359 (52.502129, -1.9804063)
Opened 25 September 1995.
WMT 4CD**HPSTT** 664,254

SMITHY BRIDGE (SMB)

Looking along Platform 1 on 28 June 2015.

Smithy Bridge, Near Rochdale, Greater Manchester OL15 0DX
SD9256815171 (53.633013, -2.1138677)
Opened by the L&YR October 1868, closed by BR 2 May 1960 and reopened 19 August 1985.
NR 2D**HPST** 167,822

SOUTHAMPTON AIRPORT PARKWAY
(SOA)
Wide Lane, Southampton SO18 2HW
SU4484116994 (50.950641, -1.3630262)
Opened by the SR 30 October 1929 as *Atlantic Park Hostel Halt*, (detraining only for emigrants to the USA) closed at an unknown date and reopened by BR 1 April 1966 *as Southampton Airport*, renamed as *Southampton Parkway for Southampton (Eastleigh) Airport* 29 September 1986, and as *Southampton Airport Parkway* 29 May 1994.
SWR 2**AB**CDHPRR**STTW** 1,842,710

SOUTHAMPTON FLYING BOAT TERMINAL
Location: SU4209510732 (50.894541, -1.4028329)
Opened 14 April 1948 and closed September 1958.

SOUTHAMPTON OCEAN TERMINAL
Location: SU4240810356 (50.891137, -1.3984287)
Opened 31 July 1950, officially closed 14 December 1991 but used again from 8 May 1994 for occasional Cunard sailings.

SOUTH BANK (SBK)

Looking east along Platform 1 on 26 September 2015 with the staggered Platform 1 in view in the distance.

Normanby Road, Middlesbrough, Redcar and Cleveland TS6 6UJ
NZ5333021288 (54.583988, -1.1763498)
Opened 23 July 1984.
NR 2C**S** 23,926

SOUTHBURY (SBU) X
Southbury Road, Enfield, Greater London EN3 4HW
TQ3483596211 (51.648536, -0.052509606)
Opened by the GER 1 October 1891 as *Churchbury*, closed 1 October 1909, reopened 1 March 1915, closed 1 July 1919 and reopened by BR 21 November 1960 as *Southbury*.
LO 2C**H**R**STT** 939,482

Looking north on 2 July 2016.

SOUTHEND AIRPORT (SIA)

Looking along Platform 1 on 12 July 2015.

Southend Airport, Essex SS4 1JD
TQ8758389116 (51.569701, 0.70531905)
Opened 18 July 2011.
SR 2C**DH**P**STTW** 395,646

SOUTH GYLE (SGL)
South Gyle Road, South Gyle, Edinburgh EH12 7XH
NT1889372273 (55.936648, -3.2999191)
Opened 9 May 1985.
ASR 2C**DH**P**ST** 497,162

SOUTH MARSTON
Location: SU1897286791 (51.579663, -1.7276055) (Approx)
Opened by the GWR 5 June 1941, closed 1944, reopened by BR 27 December 1956 and closed 30 June 1957.

SOUTH WIGSTON (SWS)
Kenilworth Road, Wigston, Leicester LE18 4XU
SP5877998643 (52.582433, -1.1339468)

Looking east along Platform 1 on 1 September 2015 with the staggered Platform 2 in view beyond the road bridge.

Opened 12 May 1986.
EMT 2CD**S** 80,180

STANHOPE

Location: NY99884 38727 (54.743507, -2.0033258)
Opened by the NER 22 October 1862, closed by BR 29 June 1953, reopened for a summer service from 22 May 1988 until 27 September 1992. Now a Heritage Railway operated by the Weardale Railway.

Looking along Platform 2 on 19 May 2016 with the staggered Platform 1 in view on the other side of the bridge.

Station Road, Keighley, West Yorkshire BD20 6RY
SE0377044854 (53.899844, -1.9441053)
Opened by the MR 28 February 1892, closed by BR 22 March 1965 and reopened 14 May 1990.
NR 2CD**H**P**S**T 851,608

Nicolson Court, Stepps, North Lanarkshire G33 6HG
NS66223 68406 (55.890144, -4.1405985)
Opened 15 May 1989.
ASR 2CD**H**P**S**T 269,880

Class 170 Unit No.170110 on Platform 2 on 12 July 2017.

Bassingbourn Road, Stansted, Essex CM24 1QW
TL5565723494 (51.888273, 0.26041567)
Opened 19 March 1991.
AGA 3A**B**CD**H**P**R**S**TT**W** 7,632,108

Looking south along Platform 2 on 30 July 2017.

Lytton Way, Stevenage, Hertfordshire SG1 1XT
TL2344924089 (51.901677, -0.20709530)
Opened 23 July 1973.
GN 4A**C**D**H**P**R**S**TT**W** 4,846,618

STEWARTON (STT)

Dunlop Road, Stewarton, East Ayrshire KA3 5BD
NS4177346044 (55.682006, -4.5181650)
Opened by the Glasgow, Barrhead & Kilmarnock Joint Railway
27 March 1871, closed by BR 7 November 1966 and reopened
5 June 1967.
ASR 2CD**HPS**T **310,602**

STOURBRIDGE TOWN (SBT)

Class 139 Unit No.139002 at the buffer stops on 28 August 2015. At
just 0.8 miles long, the Stourbridge Junction to Town branch is the
shortest on the National Rail network.

Vauxhall Road, Stourbridge, West Midlands DY8 1EX
SO9045684188 (52.455555, -2.1418753)
Opened 19 February 1979, closed 10 January 1994 and
reopened 25 April 1994.
WMT 1C**DHS**TT **575,406**

STOW (SOI)

Looking north along Platform 2 on 12 May 2017.

41 Station Road, Stow, Scottish Borders TD1 2SQ
NT4556544642 (55.692173, -2.8674799)
Opened by the NBR 1 November 1848, closed by BR 6 January
1969 and reopened 6 September 2015.
ASR 2CD**HPS**T **67,474**

STRAGEATH HALT

Location: NN8810317885 (56.340057, -3.8117314) (Approx)
Opened 15 September 1958 and closed 6 July 1964.

STRATFORD INTERNATIONAL (SFA) **X**

Looking east along Platform 3 on 4 June 2016.

International Way, Stratford, Greater London E15 2ER
TQ3820184768 (51.544894, -0.0084060431)
Opened 30 September 2009.
NetR 4A**CDHR**S**TTW** **2,135,940**

STRATFORD-UPON-AVON PARKWAY (STY)

Looking south along Platform 1 on 20 June 2015.

Bishopton Lane, Stratford-upon-Avon, Warwickshire CV37 0RJ
SP1849956534 (52.206719, -1.7307168)
Opened 19 May 2013.
WMT 2CD**HPS**T **81,084**

STREETHOUSE (SHG)

Whinney Lane, Streethouse, Pontefract,
West Yorkshire WF7 6DA
SE3975920138 (53.676203, -1.3996035)

Looking west along Platform 1 on 7 May 2016.

Opened 11 May 1992.
NR 2HPS 25,358

SUDBURY (SUFFOLK) (SUY)

Looking towards the buffer stop on 20 August 2017. This replaced the second station here, opened by the GER 9 August 1865 as *Sudbury*, renamed by the L&NER in June 1932 as *Sudbury (Suffolk)*, by BR 14 June 1965 as *Sudbury* and closed and re-sited 28 October 1990.

Station Road, Sudbury, Suffolk CO10 2RD
TL8776341071 (52.036248, 0.73603302)
Opened 28 October 1990.
AGA 1CDHPST 320,042

SUGAR LOAF (SUG)
A483, Sugar Loaf Mountain, Llanwrtyd Wells, Powys LD5 4TE
SN8458343975 (52.082061, -3.6857294)
Opened by the L&NWR in 1899 as *Sugar Loaf Summit*, closed by BR 17 November 1949, reopened 9 January 1950, closed 1965, reopened 21 July 1984, closed 25 August 1984 and reopened 25 June 1989 as *Sugar Loaf*.
ATW 1CHS 228

Looking south on 14 June 2015. It was originally built to serve four railwaymen's cottages, since demolished, and the abandoned southbound platform can be seen on the left.

SUMMERSTON (SUM)
Sandbank Street, Summerston,
Glasgow G23 5AT
NS5676369680 (55.898867, -4.2923981)
Opened 3 December 1993.
ASR 2CDHS 99,042

SUTTON PARKWAY (SPK)

Looking along Platform 1 on 3 May 2015.

Low Moor Road, Kirkby-in-Ashfield, Nottinghamshire
NG17 5LG
SK5059457707 (53.114150, -1.2455776)
Opened 20 November 1995.
EMT 2CDHPS 182,208

SWALE (SWL)

Viewed on 30 April 2017.

Sheppey Way, Sittingbourne, Kent ME9 8SS
TQ9123169151 (51.389171, 0.74708775)
Opened 20 April 1960.
SE 1CD**T 4,458**

SWINTON (SOUTH YORKS) (SWN)

Station Road, Swinton, Mexborough,
South Yorkshire S64 8AU
SK4617298996 (53.485664, -1.3056430)
Opened 14 May 1990.
NR 2CDPR**STW 395,832**

SYSTON (SYS)

Looking south on 15 August 2015.

Melton Road, Syston, Leicestershire LE7 2HA
SK6210511126 (52.694261, -1.0825101)
Opened by the Midland Counties Railway 5 May 1840, closed
4 March 1968 and reopened 28 May 1994.
EMT 1CD**PS**T **218,470**

TAME BRIDGE PARKWAY (TAB)

Looking west along Platform 1 on 17 December 2015.

Walsall Road, Friar Park, Wednesbury,
West Midlands WS10 0LD
SP0171794945 (52.552343, -1.9761094)
Opened 4 June 1990 as *Tame Bridge* and renamed 1 June 1997
as *Tame Bridge Parkway*.
WMT 2CD**HPS**TT **588,856**

TEESSIDE AIRPORT (TEA)

Looking east on 26 September 2015 with the airport to the right.

Teesside Airport, Darlington DL2 1NL
NZ3729613844 (54.518528, -1.4253661)
Opened 4 October 1971.
NR 2**HS 30**

TELFORD CENTRAL (TFC)

Looking west on 28 December 2015.

Euston Way, Telford, Shropshire TF3 4LZ
SJ7031709304 (52.680610, -2.4404964)
Opened 12 May 1986.
WMT 2CD**PRS**T**TW** 1,207,406

TEMPLECOMBE (TMC)

Looking east on 2 October 2015. Only the platform on the south side (in view on the right) is used and there is no general access to the platform on the north.

Station Road, Templecombe, Somerset BA8 0JR
ST7081622550 (51.001593, -2.4172899)
Opened by the Salisbury & Yeovil Railway 7 May 1860, closed by BR 7 March 1966 and reopened 3 October 1983.
SWR 2CD**H**P**S**T**TW** 126,676

TEVERSALL EAST*

Location: SK4779161677 (53.150097, -1.2868649) (Approx)
Opened by the GNR 1897 as *Teversall*, closed by the L&NER by May 1943, reopened by BR for excursion traffic September 1953 as *Teversall East* and closed c1968.

THE HAWTHORNS (THW)

Looking west on 27 June 2015. This station is also an interchange with the Midland Metro.

Halfords Lane, Birmingham Road, West Bromwich, West Midlands B66 2HB
SP0249889745 (52.505597, -1.9646242)
Opened by the GWR 25 December 1931 as *The Hawthorns Halt*, closed by BR 29 April 1968 and rebuilt and reopened 25 September 1995 as *The Hawthorns*.
WMT 2C**DH**P**STT** 436,562

THEOBALDS GROVE (TEO)

Looking north along Platform 1 on 27 February 2017.

High Street, Waltham Cross, Hertfordshire EN8 8AS
TL3591601104 (51.692245, -0.034994781)
Opened by the GER 1 October 1891, closed 1 October 1909, reopened 1 March 1915, closed 1 July 1919 and reopened by BR 21 November 1960.
LO 2C**H**P**RS**T**T** 413,936

THRYBERG TINS

Location: SK46536 94661 (53.446666, -1.3008043) (Approx)
Opened 17 June 1959 for excursion traffic and closed 1968.

THURNSCOE (THC)

Viewed on 16 April 2016.

Station Road, Thurnscoe, Rotherham, South Yorkshire S63 0JR
SE4592205646 (53.545449, -1.3084379)
Opened 16 May 1988.
NR 2H**PS** 76,116

TIVERTON PARKWAY (TYP)

Looking north along Platform 2 on 23 May 2017.

Sampford Peverell, Tiverton, Devon EX16 7EL
ST0449913931 (50.916911, -3.3599308)
Opened 12 May 1986.
GWR 2BCDH**PRST**T**W** 492,742

TONDU (TDU)

Station Approach, Bryn Road, Tondu, Bridgend CF32 9DE
SS8948684389 (51.547536, -3.5951874)
Opened by the Llynvi Valley Railway 25 February 1864, closed
by BR 22 June 1970 and reopened 28 September 1992.
ATW 1CD**PS** 47,226

Looking north towards the signal box on 2 August 2015. It was
originally a vee-shaped station and a junction for six lines.

TREDEGAR SOUTH END HALT
Location: SO1452308090 (51.764941, -3.2400158) (Approx)
Opened prior to September 1953 and closed 13 June 1960.

TROUBLE HOUSE HALT
Location: ST9141795346 (51.656837, -2.1254736)
Opened 2 February 1959 and closed 6 April 1964.

TURKEY STREET (TUR)

Looking along Platform 1 on 2 July 2016.

Turkey Street, Enfield, Greater London EN3 5TT
TQ3513798921 (51.672818, -0.047113001)
Opened by the GER 1 October 1891 as *Forty Hill*, closed
1 October 1909, reopened 1 March 1915, closed 1 July 1919
and reopened by BR 21 November 1960 as *Turkey Street*.
LO 2CH**ST**T 711,572

TUTBURY & HATTON (TUT)

Looking north along Platform 2 on 21 June 2015.

Station Road, Hatton, Derbyshire DE65 5DW
SK2148429680 (52.864182, -1.6823271)
Opened by the North Staffordshire Railway 11 September 1848 as *Tutbury,* closed by BR 7 November 1966 and reopened 3 April 1989 as *Tutbury and Hatton.*
EMT 2CD**HS** 68,942

TWEEDBANK (TWB)

Tweedbank Drive, Tweedbank, Galashiels,
Scottish Borders TD1 3SP
NT5227134949 (55.605796, -2.7591294)
Opened 6 September 2015.
ASR 2CD**HPS**T 436,232

TWICKENHAM (TWI) **X**

Looking west on 21 May 2016. This station replaced one opened by the Windsor, Staines and South Western Railway on 22 August 1848 which was sited 250 yards to the east.

London Road, Twickenham, Greater London TW1 3JB
TQ1616573695 (51.450330, -0.32967031)
Opened 28 March 1954.
SWR 3**AB**CDHPR**RS**TT**W** 5,924,016

TY GLAS (TGS)

Looking west on 24 May 2015.

Field Way, Maes-y-Coed Road, Cardiff CF14 5DL
ST1704480994 (51.521745, -3.1970564)
Opened 29 April 1987.
ATW I**CHS**T 204,158

UCKFIELD (UCK)

Looking towards the buffer stop on 2 October 2016. This station replaced one sited on the opposite side of the road which was opened by the Lewes & Uckfield Railway on 18 October 1858.

High Street, Uckfield, East Sussex TN22 5AD
TQ4731520910 (50.968779, 0.096669495)
Opened 13 May 1991.
So I CD**H**PRST**TW** 441,624

UNIVERSITY (BIRMINGHAM) (UNI) X

Looking west along Platform 1 on 14 February 2017.

University Road West, Edgbaston, Birmingham B15 2FG
SP0442583734 (52.451547, -1.9363108)
Opened 8 May 1978.
WMT 2C**DHS**TT **3,383,086**

UPHALL (UHA)

Station Road, Livingston, West Lothian EH54 5QE
NT0618970562 (55.918959, -3.5026056)
Opened by the Edinburgh & Bathgate Railway 12 November 1849 as *Houston*, renamed as *Uphall* by the NBR 1 August 1865, closed by BR 9 January 1956 and reopened 24 March 1986.
ASR 2CD**HP**ST **608,576**

VALLEY (VAL)

Looking north along Platform 2 on 19 July 2015.

Station Road, Valley, Holyhead, Anglesey LL65 3EW
SH2918979139 (53.281625, -4.5635614)
Opened by the Chester & Holyhead Railway c May 1849, closed by BR 14 February 1966 and reopened 15 March 1982.
ATW 2CD**HS** **15,062**

WALLINGFORD

Location: SU60220 89570 (51.601760, -1.1319119)
Opened by the Wallingford & Watlington Railway 2 July 1866, closed by BR 15 June 1959, reopened to regular passenger traffic 17 June 1967 and closed 23 September 1968.

WALLYFORD (WAF)

The Loan, Wallyford, Musselburgh, East Lothian EH21 8DZ
NT3671172405 (55.940506, -3.0147868)
Opened 13 June 1994.
ASR 2CD**HP**ST **296,996**

WALSDEN (WDN)

Looking along Platform 1 on 28 June 2015. An earlier station, sited slightly south, was opened by the Manchester and Leeds Railway in October 1845 and closed by BR 7 August 1961.

Rochdale Road, Walsden, Todmorden,
West Yorkshire OL14 6SA
SD9318722220 (53.696376, -2.1046677)
Opened 10 September 1990.
NR 2CD**S** **105,960**

WARWICK PARKWAY (WRP)

Looking south-east on 28 July 2015.

Old Budbrooke Road, Warwick CV35 7DU
SP2653365394 (52.286052, -1.6124502)
Opened 25 October 2000.
ChR 2C**DH**PR**RST**T**W** 659,428

WATER STRATFORD HALT
Location: SP6521834155 (52.002017, -1.0513884)
Opened 13 August 1956 and closed 2 January 1961.

WATFORD STADIUM
Location: TQ1023095408 (51.646672, -0.40824831)
Opened 4 December 1982 and out of use by 14 May 1993.

WATLINGTON (WTG)

Looking north along Platform 1 on 18 June 2017 with the signal box and the staggered Platform 2 in view in the distance.

Station Road, Watlington, King's Lynn, Norfolk PE33 0JF
TF6123311074 (52.673390, 0.38322866)
Opened by the Lynn & Ely Railway 27 October 1846, renamed as *Magdalen Road* by the GER 1 June 1875, closed by BR 9 September 1968, reopened 5 May 1975 and renamed as *Watlington* 3 October 1989.
GN 2C**DH**P**ST** 144,114

WATTON-AT-STONE (WAS)

Viewed on 30 July 2017.

Station Road, Watton-at-Stone, Hertfordshire SG14 3SH
TL2958719248 (51.856785, -0.11975259)
Opened by the L&NER 2 June 1924, closed 11 September 1939 and reopened by BR 17 May 1982.
GN 2C**H**P**STT** 167,752

WAUN-GRON PARK (WNG)

Viewed on 24 May 2015.

Waungron Road, Cardiff CF5 2JL
ST1472577305 (51.488238, -3.2295808)
Opened 2 November 1987.
ATW 2C**DST** 88,652

WAVERTREE TECHNOLOGY PARK (WAV)

Looking west along Platform 2 on 11 September 2016.

Rathbone Road, Liverpool L15 4HH
SJ3874690228 (53.405298, -2.9228380)
Opened 13 August 2000.
NR 2C**DH**P**ST** 533,490

WELHAM GREEN (WMG)

Looking north along Platform 1 on 23 July 2017.

Dixons Hill Lane, Welham Green, North Hatfield,
Hertfordshire AL9 7JA
TL2369505653 (51.735949, -0.21010011)
Opened 29 September 1986.
GN 2C**HPS**T**T 213,534**

WELSHPOOL (WLP)

Looking north along Platform 1 on 18 February 2015. This station was built following the realignment of the trackbed to accommodate construction of the A483 Welshpool by-pass and the original station building is still extant as a Tourist Centre (*Allison Smith*).

Off A483, Welshpool, Powys SY21 7AY
SJ2299307263 (52.657598, -3.1399038)
Opened 18 May 1992.
ATW 2CD**HPS**T **170,648**

WEST BROMPTON (WBP) **X**
Lillie Road, Fulham, London SW5 9JX
TQ2537778007 (51.487122, -0.19563764)
Opened by the West London Extension Railway 1 September 1866, closed 21 October 1940 and rebuilt and reopened 30 May 1999.
LU 2C**DHS**T**T 5,226,416**

Looking north on 6 August 2016.

WESTER HAILES (WTA)
Wester Hailes Road, Wester Hailes, Edinburgh EH14 3JH
NT1986169782 (55.914432, 55.914432)
Opened 11 May 1987.
ASR 2CD**HPS 36,080**

WEST HAM (WEH)

Looking west along Platform 8 on 14 May 2016. The platforms on the right are for London Underground services.

Manor Road, London E15 3BN
TQ3925182984 (51.528607, 0.0060215592)
Opened by the London Tilbury & Southend Railway 1 February 1901 and renamed as *West Ham Manor Road* by the LM&SR 11 February 1924. The District Line started using the station from 2 June 1902 and the Metropolitan from 30 June 1936 and when the station was closed due to bomb damage from 7 September 1940 until 11 August 1941, the LM&SR platforms were removed. It was renamed as *West Ham* 1 January 1969 and the ex-LM&SR platforms were rebuilt and reopened 30 May 1999.
LU 2C**DHS**T**T 10,629,626**

WEST HAM (LOW LEVEL)
Location: TQ3915182870 (51.527603, 0.0045409799)
Opened by BR 14 May 1979, closed 29 May 1994, reopened 29 October 1995 and closed 9 December 2006 for conversion to DLR.

WEST HOATHLY
Location: TQ3713732851 (51.078603, -0.043674409)
Opened by the Lewes & East Grinstead Railway 1 August 1882, closed by BR 30 May 1955, reopened 7 August 1956, after legal objections, and closed 17 March 1958.

WETHERAL (WRL)

Looking north-east along Platform 2 on 19 September 2015.

Off Steele's Bank, Wetheral, Carlisle, Cumbria CA4 8LH
NY4673554649 (54.883739, -2.8317824)
Opened by the Newcastle and Carlisle Railway 19 July 1836, closed by BR 2 January 1967 and reopened 5 October 1981.
NR 2HPS 22,872

WHALLEY (LANCS) (WHE)

Viewed on 31 May 2015.

The Sidings, Station Road, Whalley, Lancashire BB7 9RT
SD7297636533 (53.824355, -2.4120060)
Opened by the Bolton, Blackburn, Clitheroe and West Yorkshire Railway 22 June 1850, closed by BR 10 September 1962 and reopened 29 May 1994.
NR 2HPS 83,182

WHIFFLET (WFF)
Easton Place, Whifflet, North Lanarkshire ML5 4EE
NS7373964131 (55.853794, -4.0185231)
Opened 21 December 1992.
ASR 2CDHPST 329,588

WHINHILL (WNL)
Riverside Road, Whinhill, Greenock, Inverclyde PA15 3AQ
NS2853975119 (55.938451, -4.7467080)
Opened 14 May 1990.
ASR 1CDHS 43,696

WHISTON (WHN)
Pennywood Drive, Whiston, Prescot,
Merseyside L35 3TY
SJ4714891084 (53.413903, -2.7966186)
Opened 1 October 1990.
NR 2DHST 367,130

WHITWELL (DERBYSHIRE) (WWL)

Looking along Platform 1 on 3 May 2015.

Station Road, Whitwell, Worksop, Derbyshire S80 4TA
SK5344476202 (53.280111, -1.1999211)
Opened by the MR 1 June 1875, closed by BR 12 October 1964 and rebuilt and reopened 25 May 1998.
EMT 2CDHPS 20,376

WILDMILL (WMI)
Wildmill Lane, Bridgend CF31 1RW
SS9045681298 (51.519948, -3.5802408)

Looking south on 2 August 2015.

Opened 16 November 1992, closed same day (due to wrongly-sited shelter) and reopened 12 December 1992.
ATW 1D**HS** **25,414**

WILLINGTON (WIL)

Looking along Platform 1 on 26 December 2015.

The Green, Willington, Derbyshire DE65 6BP
SK2946228529 (52.853454, -1.5639237)
Opened by the Birmingham & Derby Junction Railway 12 August 1839, renamed as *Willington and Repton* by the MR 1 October 1855, as *Repton and Willington* 1 May 1877, closed by BR 4 March 1968 and reopened as *Willington* 29 May 1995.
EMT 2C**HPS** **31,522**

WINCHESTER CHESIL

Location: SU4876329222 (51.060272, -1.3055572)
Opened by the Didcot, Newbury & Southampton Railway on 4 May 1885 as *Winchester Cheesehill*, closed by the SR 4 August 1942, reopened 8 March 1943, renamed as *Winchester Chesil* by BR 26 September 1949, closed 7 March 1960. It was reopened 18 June 1960, closed 10 September 1960, reopened 17 June 1961 and closed 9 September 1961 for summer Saturday holiday traffic.

WINDERMERE (WDM)

Looking towards the buffer stop on 26 April 2016. The original station was opened by the Kendal & Windermere Railway 21 April 1847 and closed when the line was truncated in 1986.

Station Precinct, Windermere, Cumbria LA23 1AH
SD4138998648 (54.379936, -2.9038748)
Opened 17 April 1986.
NR 1CD**HPSTTW** **415,448**

WINNERSH TRIANGLE (WTI)

Looking along Platform 1 on 16 April 2017.

Wharfedale Road, Winnersh Triangle, Wokingham, Berkshire RG41 5TS
SU7714171439 (51.436711, -0.89160115)
Opened 12 May 1986.
SWR 2C**HPSTT** **469,354**

WITTON PARK

Location: NZ1748230251 (54.667038, -1.7304706)
Opened by the NER as *Etherley and Witton Park* by 16 October 1867, renamed as *Etherley* 1 July 1871, closed by BR 8 March 1965, reopened as *Witton Park* 25 August 1991 and closed 27 September 1992.

WOODSMOOR (WSR)
Moorland Road, Stockport, Greater Manchester SK2 7AX
SJ9069487715 (53.386195, -2.1413764)
Opened 1 October 1990.
NR 2**ST** 253,746

WORLE (WOR)

Looking east along Platform 2 on 25 September 2016.

Station Approach, Worle, Weston super Mare, North
Somerset BS22 6WA
ST3679262486 (51.357914, -2.9091588)
Opened 24 September 1990.
GWR 2**DHPST**T 321,306

WORSBOROUGH BRIDGE
Location: SE3519503615 (53.528020, -1.4705506)
Opened for works outings only prior to July 1965 and closed
after 1968.

WREXHAM CENTRAL (WXC)

Viewed on 17 May 2015. It opened when the original station, sited 400
yards to the east and opened by the Cambrian and Wrexham, Mold &
Connah's Quay Railways 1 November 1887, was demolished to make
way for a shopping development.

Hill Street, Wrexham LL11 1SN
SJ3306250374 (53.046418, -2.9999354)
Opened 23 November 1998.
ATW 1**CDHPS**T 74,184

YARM (YRM)

Class 185 Unit No.185118 on Platform 2 on 26 September 2015. A
previous station, sited to the north, was opened by the Leeds Northern
Railway 2 June 1852 and closed by BR 4 January 1960.

Green Lane, Yarm, Cleveland TS15 9EQ
NZ4209911145 (54.493898, -1.3515598)
Opened 19 February 1996.
TPE 2**CDHPS**T 147,058

YATE (YAE)

Looking north on 7 June 2015 with the former Thornbury branch, in
use for freight, visible diverging to the left.

Badminton Road, Yate, South Gloucestershire BS37 4PS
ST7010882543 (51.540990, -2.4324122)
Opened by the Birmingham and Gloucester Railway 8 July 1844,
closed by BR 4 January 1965 and rebuilt and reopened 15 May
1989.
GWR 2**DHPST**T 392,910

YNYSWEN (YNW)

Class 150 Unit No.150251 on a service to Treherbert on 10 May 2015. This station is built on the site of *Tylacoch* which was opened by the Taff Vale Railway c October 1906 and closed c November 1912.

Ynyswen Road, Ynyswen, Treorchy CF42 6ED
SS9486697345 (51.665013, -3.5215178)
Opened 29 September 1986.
ATW 1CD**HS 13,346**

YSTRAD RHONDDA (YSR)

Looking north-west on 10 May 2015. The name of this station is alphabetically the last in the National Rail list.

Brook Street, Ystrad, Pentre, Rhondda Cynon Taff CF41 7RB
SS9856694906 (51.643776, -3.4673291)
Opened 29 September 1986.
ATW 2C**HPS 56,398**

STAFF HALTS & TEMPORARY STATIONS

ACHTERNEED
Location: NH4901659794 (57.602815, -4.5283483)
Opened 19 August 1870 by the HR as *Strathpeffer*, renamed 1 June 1885 as *Achterneed* and closed 7 December 1964 by BR. It was reopened 8 February 1965 as an unadvertised and unstaffed halt. Date of final closure not recorded.

BULMER'S SIDINGS
Used 24 April 1971 for an open day.

CARLISLE UPPERBY
A temporary station pending rebuilding of roadbridge. Opened 2 April 1994 and closed 4 April 1994.

CHEE DALE HALT
Location: SK1105572611 (53.250397, -1.8357811)
Opened 5 July 1987, closed 13 September 1987. A halt for ramblers closed by H&SE due to poor line signalling.

CILCEWYDD EAST
Assumed Location: SJ2282704080 (52.628968, -3.1416097)
Temporary station pending bridge strengthening. Opened 17 January 1994 and closed 26 February 1994.

CILCEWYDD WEST
Assumed Location: SJ2278404379 (52.631650, -3.1423187)
Temporary station pending bridge strengthening. Opened 17 January 1994 and closed 26 February 1994.

CULROSS
Location: NS98333 85856 (56.054725, -3.6340472)
Opened by the NBR 2 July 1906 and closed 7 July 1930. Reopened in connection with the town's centenary celebrations 21 June 1992 to 22 June 1992 and 1 August 1992 to 2 August 1992.

EASTFIELD DEPOT
Used for open days 16 and 17 September 1972.

GLOUCESTER OVER BRIDGE
Temporary terminus set up due to flooding west of Gloucester. Opened 6 February 1990 and closed 21 February 1990.

HAYMARKET TMD
Used on open days for trains from Waverley. Dates unknown but definitely 24 August 1984.

HEATHROW JUNCTION
Location: TQ0770979373 (51.503035, -0.44958063)
A temporary terminus opened 19 January 1998 after collapse of the tunnel into the airport and closed 25 May 1998.

HOO JUNCTION STAFF HALT
Location: [Down platform] TQ69601 73647 (51.436437, 0.43867466), [Up platform] TQ69965 73585 (51.435772, 0.44387814)
Opened 6 February 1956 and out of use by 2002.

IMMINGHAM MOTIVE POWER DEPOT
Opened on unknown date for a Sunday open day, closed after September 1974.

LANDORE DEPOT
Used for an open day on 30 August 1980.

LENTRAN
Location: NH5842145802 (57.480282, -4.3629724)
Opened by the Inverness & Ross-shire Railway 11 June 1862, closed by BR 13 June 1960, reopened as a temporary terminus during the period 27 March 1982 – 29 March 1982 when the swing bridge at Clachnaharry was being repaired.

LONGSIGHT
Location: SJ8681495927 (53.459925, -2.2000656)
Opened March 1980 for railway personnel and became a temporary station for public use during remodelling of Manchester Piccadilly station between 23 July 1989 and 17 October 1989. It reverted to railway use only and has since been abandoned.

NEWTON ABBOT GOODS DEPOT
Opened for an exhibition between 24 July 1980 and 31 July 1980.

OLD OAK COMMON
Opened for depot open days 15 July 1967 as *Old Oak Platform for Diesel Depot* and renamed as *Old Oak Common* by September 1981. Probably closed 1991.

PRESTON MAUDLANDS
A temporary station opened during bridge rebuilding between 9 March 1991 and 10 March 1991.

RAF FILLINGLEY HALT
Used on 19 September 1981 and 20 September 1981.

READING CENTRAL
Used for open days 19 June 1971 and 20 June 1971.

READING DIESEL DEPOT
Used for open days 19 June 1971 and 20 June 1971.

REDDISH DEPOT
Used for open day 9 September 1973.

SHIELDS DEPOT
Used for open day 16 September 1978.

SUDBROOK
Used 12 August 1978 for excursion to Barry by Sudbrook Non-Political Club.

TINSLEY YARD HALT
Used for open day 15 June 1980.

TRAWSFYNYDD POWER STATION
Opened 15 July 1990 and closed 9 September 1990.

TURNCHAPEL
Location: SX4973252978 (50.357479, -4.1138303)
Opened by the L&SWR on 5 September 1892, closed by BR 15 January 1951, reopened 2 July 1951 and closed 10 September 1951.

UPPERBY PLANT & MACHINERY WORKSHOP
Used for open days 5 July 1980 and 7 July 1980.

WORKINGTON NORTH
Location: NX9967830294 (54.657723, -3.5566252)
Temporary station used after severe flooding destroyed bridges over the River Derwent. Opened 30 November 2009 and closed 8 October 2010.

STATIONS UNDER CONSTRUCTION, APPROVED OR PROPOSED AS AT 1 JANUARY 2018

ADDENBROOKE'S – Proposed for completion by 2011

BALSALL HEATH (BIRMINGHAM) – Proposal for reopening

BARKING RIVERSIDE – Approved for opening in 2021

BIRMINGHAM CURZON STREET – An HS2 station opening in 2026

BIRMINGHAM INTERCHANGE – An HS2 station opening in 2026

BOND STREET – A Crossrail 1 station opening in 2018/19

BOW STREET (WALES) – Approved in July 2017

BRIERLEY HILL (WEST MIDLANDS) – Proposal for reopening

CANARY WHARF – A Crossrail 1 station opening in 2018/19

CHERRY HINTON – Proposal for reopening

CUSTOM HOUSE – A Crossrail 1 station opening in 2018/19

DALCROSS – Under construction with projected opening date in 2019

DARLASTON (WEST MIDLANDS) – Proposal for reopening

EAST LINTON – Proposal for reopening in 2021

EDGINSWELL – Construction commencing in summer 2018 for opening in Spring 2019

ELLAND (WEST YORKSHIRE) – Proposed

FULBOURN – Proposal for reopening

HAZELWELL (BIRMINGHAM) – Proposal for reopening

HEADBOLT LANE (KNOWSLEY) – Proposed

HORDEN PETERLOO – Proposed opening in March 2020

HYTHE ROAD (LONDON) – Proposed

KENILWORTH – Reopened 30 April 2018

KINGS HEATH (BIRMINGHAM) – Proposal for reopening

KINTORE – Under construction, projected reopening in 2019

LEEDS BRADFORD INTERNATIONAL AIRPORT PARKWAY (WEST YORKSHIRE) – Proposed

MAGHULL NORTH – Opened 18 June 2018

MARSH BARTON – Construction currently stalled due to lack of finance

MERIDIAN WATER – Under construction with projected opening date in 2019

MOSELEY (BIRMINGHAM) – Proposal for reopening

OLD OAK COMMON – An HS2 station opening in 2026

OLD OAK COMMON LANE – Proposed

PORTWAY PARKWAY – Approved in July 2017

READING GREEN PARK – Approved in July 2017

RESTON – Proposal for reopening in 2021

ROBROYSTON – Proposal for reopening in March 2019

RUGBY PARKWAY – Approved. Due to open in December 2019

SKELMERSDALE – Proposed

SOHAM – Proposal for reopening in 2022

STEEPLE CLAYDON – Proposed

THORPE PARK (WEST YORKSHIRE) – Proposed

TOTTENHAM COURT ROAD – A Crossrail 1 station opening in 2018/19

WARRINGTON WEST – Approved in July 2017

WATERLOO INTERNATIONAL – Due to reopen as part of Waterloo Station during 2018

WHITE ROSE (WEST YORKSHIRE) – Proposed

WILLENHALL (WEST MIDLANDS) – Proposal for reopening

WINSLOW – Proposal for opening on new site. Projected opening date in 2019

WOOLWICH – A Crossrail 1 station opening in 2018/19

WORCESTERSHIRE PARKWAY REGIONAL INTERCHANGE – Under construction, projected opening in Winter 2018

BIBLIOGRAPHY

BEVAN, Alan *A-Z of Rail Re-Openings*. Railway Development Society (March 1988)

BUTT R.V.J. *The Directory of Railway Stations*. Patrick Stephens Ltd.

CLINKER C.R. *Clinker's Register of Closed Passenger Stations & Goods Depots in England, Scotland and Wales 1830-1980*. Avon Anglia Publications. Second Edition. (1988)

QUICK M. *Railway Passenger Stations in Great Britain: A Chronology*. Railway & Canal Historical Society (2009)

SMITH P. & TURNER K. *Railway Atlas, Then & Now*. Ian Allan Publishing. Second Edition. (2015)

WIGNALL C.J. *Complete British Railways Maps & Gazetteer 1825-1985*. Oxford Publishing Company.

ACKNOWLEDGEMENTS

With grateful thanks to Dermot Buckley (Royal Marines) and staff at the SSI Plant, Redcar, for organising access to Lympstone Commando and Redcar British Steel stations respectively. To John Ledward for transporting us around southern England to photograph some of the stations and to Nick Pigott, Peter Waller and members of the Engine Shed Society, for their assistance in compiling and dating some of the temporary stations.